How Bad Writing Destroyed the World

How Bad Writing Destroyed the World

Ayn Rand and the Literary Origins of the Financial Crisis

Adam Weiner

Bloomsbury Academic

An imprint of Bloomsbury Publishing Inc

B L O O M S B U R Y

NEW YORK • LONDON • OXFORD • NEW DELHI • SYDNEY

Bloomsbury Academic

An imprint of Bloomsbury Publishing Inc

1385 Broadway	50 Bedford Square
New York	London
NY 10018	WC1B 3DP
USA	UK

www.bloomsbury.com

**BLOOMSBURY and the Diana logo are trademarks
of Bloomsbury Publishing Plc**

First published 2016

Library of Congress Cataloging-in-Publication Data
Names: Weiner, Adam, author.
Title: How bad writing destroyed the world : Ayn Rand and the literary
origins of the financial crisis / Adam Weiner.
Description: New York : Bloomsbury Academic, 2016. | Includes bibliographical
references and index.
Identifiers: LCCN 2016012074| ISBN 9781501313110 (pbk. : alk. paper) |
ISBN 9781501313127 (epub)
Subjects: LCSH: Russian literature–Influence. | Rationalism in literature. |
Egoism in literature. | Russian literature–Moral and ethical aspects. |
Chernyshevsky, Nikolay Gavrilovich, 1828-1889. Chto delat§? |
Chernyshevsky, Nikolay Gavrilovich, 1828-1889–Influence. | Dostoyevsky,
Fyodor, 1821-1881–Influence. | Rand, Ayn. | Economics and
literature–United States. | Russian literature–Economic aspects.
Classification: LCC PG2987.R3 W45 2016 | DDC 891.709–dc23 LC
record available at https://lccn.loc.gov/2016012074

ISBN: PB: 978-1-5013-1311-0
ePDF: 978-1-5013-1313-4
ePub: 978-1-5013-1312-7

Cover design: Alice Marwick

Typeset by Deanta Global Publishing Services, Chennai, India
Printed and bound in the United States of America

For Jenette

Contents

Introduction: On the dubious virtue of selfishness

The loaves of knowledge do not come nicely sliced.
All you get is a stone-strewn field to plough on
an exhilarating morning.[1]

VLADIMIR NABOKOV

The ideas of economists and political philosophers, both
when they are right and when they are wrong, are more
powerful than is commonly understood. Indeed the world is
ruled by little else. Practical men, who believe themselves to
be exempt from any intellectual influences, are usually the
slaves of some defunct economist.[2]

JOHN MAYNARD KEYNES

Many would be surprised to learn that classic Russian literature offers special insight into the ongoing American economic crisis. In a very real way, this crisis derives from a "defunct economist," a man who is all but forgotten today, especially outside Russian borders. Nikolai Chernyshevsky (1828–89) was one of the great destructive influences of the past two centuries. His philosophy of "rational egoism," as he presented it in his history-shaping novel *What Is to Be Done? Some Stories about the New People* (1863), would later become the foundation of Ayn Rand's objectivism. At first glance this is surprising since Chernyshevsky is Russia's great native socialist and Rand our very own arch-capitalist: it would seem that there must be a flaw either in the logic of rational egoism or in the logic of objectivism—or in both. But then logic, which both Chernyshevsky and Rand claimed as central to their philosophy, can create different, even antithetical, results, depending upon its premises. The claim being made in all seriousness is that the rational pursuit of selfish gain on the part of each individual must give rise to the ideal form of society. Odd: the very combination of the words "rational" and "egoism" should summon up grave doubts in those who have felt egoism and possessed sufficient rational sense to calculate its effects. Experience teaches quite the opposite: reason immediately abandons the mind of a person in pursuit of selfish ends. To say that all of this is naïve is to put it charitably— though, ironically, Chernyshevsky's system, like Rand's, strictly forbids charity. The deep logic that drives both systems is that of behavioral conditioning. By programming Alan Greenspan with objectivism and, literally, walking him into the highest circles of government, Rand had effectively chucked a ticking time bomb into the boiler room of the US economy. I am choosing my metaphor deliberately: as I will show, infiltration and bomb-throwing were revolutionary methods that shaped the tradition upon which Rand was consciously or unconsciously drawing.

While I do not want to equate Lenin's bloody repression with the economic devastation Greenspan caused as chairman of the Federal Reserve, I will observe that human suffering is a real possibility when "robots" programmed with ideas from destructive books are released upon reality.

How could such folly have become reality—twice? It happened through a combination of bad writers, bad readers, and bad luck. Bad luck, in particular, plays a central role in this story. In this regard Chernyshevsky's case is astounding. Imprisoned for sedition in 1862 in the Peter and Paul Fortress in St. Petersburg, he asked for permission to write a novel. For some reason the prison warden granted him permission. The book turned out to be *What Is to Be Done?*—a thinly disguised training manual for revolutionaries. Next the tsar's censor allowed the novel to be published on the pages of the widely read journal, *The Contemporary*, which, under Chernyshevsky's editorship, had become a hotbed of radicalism. The censor had apparently reasoned that the novel was so dreadfully written that it could only hurt the radical cause: fateful miscalculation. Finally, Nikolai Nekrasov, the great Russian poet and editor of *The Contemporary*, forgot the only copy of Chernyshevsky's manuscript in his horse-drawn cab. This should have saved humanity from the consequences of Chernyshevsky's book, but Nekrasov published a note about the lost manuscript in the paper, and against all odds it was soon returned to him by—of all people—a policeman.

Still, the most surprising part of this story is not attributable to luck. Some devastating algorithm of Chernyshevsky's novel became very effective at converting people into terrorists. The novel, once published, did not merely arouse spasms of sarcastic laughter (it did that too); it somehow became the cherished book of the next three generations, a catechism for educated young people. The famous Marxist revolutionary Georgy Plekhanov thought the book so important that he published a monograph on it in 1910, arguing that it was an artistic failure but a great source of inspiration for the Russian revolutionary movement. Beyond that, it also established a paradigm for behavior and social interaction immediately in the 1860s and for several generations to come. Irina Paperno paints a colorful picture of this paradigm in her seminal study of Chernyshevsky, where she argues that his "most significant act was the creation of a unified model of behavior for the age of realism, the conception of a new type of personality, with a different orientation to the world and different patterns of behavior, that contemporaries eagerly adopted."[3] *What Is to Be Done?* became a "new Gospel" to its adherents, for whom it was "a program of conduct carried out with the kind of piety and zeal inspired in the proselytes of a new religion."[4] The literary critic Alexander Skabichevsky was in his mid-twenties when Chernyshevsky's novel appeared, and he later recalled its popularity among the intelligentsia:

> We read the novel almost like worshippers, with the kind of piety with which we read religious books, and without the slightest trace of a smile on our lips. The influence of the novel on our society was colossal. It played a great role in Russian life, especially among the leading members of the intelligentsia who were embarking on the road to socialism,

bringing it down a bit from the world of drama to the problem of our social evils, sharpening its image as the goal which each of us had to fight for.[5]

Mikhail Katkov, the editor of the journal *Russkii vestnik (The Russian Messenger)*, wrote that young people in the 1860s worshipped Chernyshevsky's novel "like Moslems honor the Koran."[6] This new religion, while built upon a foundation of determinism, indulged its followers with the idea of endless personal freedom by depicting again and again an almost miraculous process of transformation by which socially inept people became like aristocrats, prostitutes became honest workers, and hack writers became literary giants.[7] In imitation of Chernyshevsky's fictional heroes, young men would enter into fictitious marriages with young women in order to liberate them from their oppressive families. The nominal husband and wife would obey Chernyshevsky's rules of communal living, with private rooms for everybody and sexual relations by mutual consent. In imitation of the sewing cooperative in Chernyshevsky's novel, communes began sprouting all over the place.[8] The imitators of Chernyshevsky's heroes, especially of his superman, Rakhmetov, would eventually include extremists like Vera Zasulich, Nikolai Ishutin, Dmitry Karakozov, Sergei Nechaev, and Alexander and Vladimir Ulyanov (Lenin).

Fyodor Dostoevsky was a mawkish and second-rate writer in 1863, but grasping the apocalyptic potential of *What Is to Be Done?*, he was compelled to reinvent himself as a brilliantly innovative novelists in order to fight Chernyshevsky and the westernizing trend he represented. Dostoevsky's first great work of literature, *Notes from the Underground* (1864), was a direct response to Chernyshevsky's novel. His four classic novels, *Crime and Punishment* (1866), *The Idiot* (1868), *The Devils* (1872), and *The Brothers Karamazov* (1880), build upon the stylistic discoveries made, so to speak, in the laboratory of the underground. For much of the remainder of his life, Dostoevsky continued to ridicule Chernyshevsky's ideals, attempting to replace them with a mystical religious alternative he would come to call the "Russian Idea." The decade that followed the publication of *What Is to Be Done?* witnessed a strange race between life and literature, as Dostoevsky kept trying to stomp out the revolutionary fire, while the living imitators of Rakhmetov kept lighting new ones. Dostoevsky died, and the fire spread out of control. Lenin read *What Is to Be Done?* and was reborn an austere, uncompromising, real-life Rakhmetov. He would go on to lead the Russian Revolution and authorize the Red Terror, bequeathing an apparatus and methodology of repression to Stalin.

Having escaped the Red Terror, Nabokov spent twenty years in Europe, writing under the pen name of V. Sirin and becoming the greatest novelist of the Russian diaspora. The last novel Nabokov wrote in Russian is his farewell to Russian literature, *The Gift* (1937). At the heart of *The Gift* is an eccentric biography of Chernyshevsky that is meant to contain and neutralize the harmful influence of *What Is to Be Done?* Nabokov's novel is an exorcism by satire: Chernyshevsky was a materialist but he did not know nature; he raised the blind worship of material things to a spiritual level. Nor does Nabokov spare Dostoevsky, whom he portrays in a ludicrous light in his encounter with Chernyshevsky. From Nabokov's point of view Chernyshevsky and Dostoevsky were both hacks because they favored ideology over artistic considerations. Chernyshevsky's communist utopia and Dostoevsky's Christian one are both rubbish. According to Nabokov's aesthetic, a good writer strives first for perfect form, which in turn chooses its own content; and art must be created according to its own standards rather than bent to the artist's ideology; otherwise it is mere propaganda. Nabokov's ingenious novel was, of course, bypassed by history.

Ayn Rand had grown up as Alisa Rosenbaum in Dostoevsky and Nabokov's beloved St. Petersburg. By virtue of some whimsical plotting on the part of fate, she had played as a small child with Nabokov's sisters at the Nabokov mansion. She grew up at a time when Chernyshevsky's influence was ubiquitous and unassailable, when it was one of the Russian intelligentsia's cherished pastimes to imitate Chernyshevsky's literary characters and attempt to incarnate his ideas in their own life and flesh. While justifiably terrified of the Revolution and loathing its ideals, the brooding young Rosenbaum had taken on board the rational egoism and superheroism of one of its chief plotters. It was with this contraband that Rosenbaum fled to the United States in 1926, rebranding herself Ayn Rand. Even as Nabokov was trying to drive a stake through Chernyshevsky's heart, Rand was raising Chernyshevsky from the dead in the graveyard of bad ideas. She would resurrect his rational egoism, his zealous belief that, in Rand's words, "form follows purpose" in art, and, most importantly, his image of the fictional hero as uncompromising revolutionary "rigorist," or, as Rand put it, "the extremist."[9]

It is strange to think that Nabokov was at work on *The Gift* during the very years when Ayn Rand was writing *The Fountainhead* (1943), her first big literary success. Both would soon be enormously popular American novelists. Nabokov's examination of the legacy of Chernyshevsky gave him the idea to ensnare him in a book, transforming him from an uncontrollable historical force to a manageable literary character. Rand was doing just the opposite, resurrecting Chernyshevsky in order to spring him anew upon the world. Nabokov immigrated to the United States in 1940, and never seems to have intersected with Rand on American soil. William F. Buckley Jr. started his campaign against rational egoism and its aftereffects where his friend Nabokov had left off. Buckley's relationship with Ayn Rand over the decades, though not entirely devoid of friendly feelings, was strained and awkward. As two leaders of the conservative movement who mostly agreed on economic matters, they might have been allies, but a chill entered their relations from the very start, when, according to Buckley, Rand scolded him that he was "too intelligent to believe in God."[10] When Rand broke with Buckley, she alienated herself from the conservative movement, blundering into increasingly strange ideological terrain, where she became subject to the delusions of cultish isolation and foolishly magnified her importance. In the early 1950s she was reading aloud from the manuscript of *Atlas Shrugged* to her acolytes in "The Collective," as Alan Greenspan and the others who made up Rand's coterie called themselves, and by now she was too far gone in self-aggrandizement to be capable of responding to criticism. It was perhaps out of a higher principle than mere revenge lust that Buckley asked Whittaker Chambers to review *Atlas Shrugged* for *The National Review*. Buckley later commented, "I believe she died under the impression that I had done it to punish her for her faithlessness," but he maintained that it was not a hit piece he had asked Chambers to write.[11]

In any case, Chambers responded by writing "Big Sister Is Watching You." He called *Atlas Shrugged* "a remarkably silly book," a "ferro-concrete fairy tale" in which all characters are either caricatures of good or caricatures of evil.[12] The novel, wrote Chambers, describes a war between the "Children of Dark" and the "Children of Light." The Children of Dark are all "looters," that is "base, envious, twisted, malignant minds, motivated wholly by greed for power, combined with the lust of the weak to tear down the strong, out of a deep-seated hatred of life and secret longing for destruction and death." The Children of Light are superhuman characters who triumph over the collectivist looters by declaring a capital strike. Chambers mistrusts Rand's rearrangement of the world, which she hands over to the inventors, engineers, and industrialists, and Chambers' best insight is that it is precisely Rand's tedious, grating "dictatorial tone" that unmasks her as "big sister." And truly, the essential core of both Chernyshevsky's and Rand's thought is not socialism or capitalism but the tyrannical will to control humanity and shape its destiny.

Out of a lifetime of reading, I can recall no other book in which a tone of overriding arrogance was so implacably sustained. Its shrillness is without reprieve. Its dogmatism is without appeal. In addition, the mind which finds this tone natural to it shares other characteristics of its type. 1) It consistently mistakes raw force for strength, and the rawer the force, the more reverent the posture of the mind before it. 2) It supposes itself to be the bringer of a final revelation. Therefore, resistance to the Message cannot be tolerated because disagreement can never be merely honest, prudent, or just humanly fallible. Dissent from revelation so final (because, the author would say, so reasonable) can only be willfully wicked. There are ways of dealing with such wickedness, and, in fact, right reason itself enjoins them. From almost any page of *Atlas Shrugged*, a voice can be heard, from painful necessity, commanding: "To a gas chamber—go!"

Rand never forgave Buckley this review, which she pretended not to have read; her followers, he claimed, were forbidden from so much as mentioning it.[13] Buckley, in a television interview, described *Atlas Shrugged* as "a thousand pages of ideological fabulism" and chuckled that he had had to "flog" himself to read it.[14] He periodically called Rand up on the phone in an attempt to make peace. She would pick up the phone, listen for a second, utter, "You are drunk!" and hang up in disgust.[15] In an evilly gloating obituary Buckley announced in 1982 that Ayn Rand's "stillborn" philosophy had died with its author.[16] He was wrong: in 1982 Ayn Rand's thought was in fact only gathering steam. Alan Greenspan would soon be transforming Rand's "stillborn" ideas into "zombie" policy.

If Chernyshevsky awakened Lenin, then Ayn Rand did the same for Alan Greenspan. "I was intellectually limited until I met her," wrote Greenspan: "Rand persuaded me to look at human beings, their values, how they work, what they do and why they do it, and how they think and why they think. This broadened my horizons far beyond the models of economics I'd learned."[17] I want to pause to take in this picture of Alan Greenspan studying "human beings" in order to learn their ways. Rand first cowed Greenspan, then groomed him, converting him from a self-proclaimed "logical positivist" to one of her most loyal objectivists. Upon publication of Chambers' review, it was Greenspan who took it upon himself to write a letter of sycophantic protest to Buckley, complaining, "This man is beneath contempt and I would not honor his 'review' of Ayn Rand's magnificent masterpiece by even commenting on it."[18] This was just the sort of loyalty that Rand demanded and rewarded. Having reprogrammed Greenspan, she accompanied him (and his biological mother) to the White House, where he was sworn in as the president's chief economist. Disappointed that her novels, particularly *Atlas Shrugged*, had failed to transform reality into an objectivist paradise, Rand had created in Alan Greenspan a final devastating hero, heir to Rakhmetov, heir to John Galt, and freed him from her pages that he might operate unfettered in the medium of history. Greenspan was the flesh of her mind, her idea incarnate, and she must have wanted to live through him, as he began to wield objectivism, first in the White House, after her death in the Federal Reserve, where he would offer up the US economy in a spectacular hecatomb.

With his Randian belief in a free marketplace, regulated only by the self-interest and rational business decisions of capitalists, Greenspan deregulated the market during the 1990s and early 2000s. But deregulation was only one half of his policy; the other half directly contradicted the principle behind deregulation: the manipulation of markets through the infamous "Greenspan Put." Deregulation led to speculative "bubbles," which would invariably "pop," but when stocks began to crash, Greenspan would lower the *fed fund rate*, flooding the market with liquidity. Eventually these interventions led to a belief that Greenspan would never allow a real crash, or, to put that differently, would never allow a free market. The result was "moral hazard," that is, traders making increasingly risky bets with full faith in bailouts should the trades "blow up." This self-contradictory policy ushered in the current cycle of bubbles, busts, and bailouts. A federal inquiry placed the blame for the economic crisis squarely at Greenspan's feet. Rigged up as policy and put into practice in the United States, objectivism has led its servants into a quagmire of contradictions: socialist welfare bestowed upon giant insolvent corporations and capitalistic austerity inflicted upon the underclasses. To be fair, Ayn Rand claimed to abominate crony capitalism and would perhaps have objected to bailouts for "too big to fail" corporations. Yet the fundamental flaw was in Rand's system. Her disciple Greenspan, by deregulating the markets, just as she had taught him, created conditions that inevitably gave an unfair advantage to the largest corporations.

In *The Wealth of Nations* (1776) Adam Smith posited an "invisible hand" that guides the selfishly motivated individual to make decisions that benefit society as a whole. Rational egoism, objectivism, and the economic policy of the Greenspan era take this notion out of context, combine it with a fervent belief in the rationality of decision makers in the economic sphere, and arrive at a uniquely destructive dogma. Putting all of his trust in this invisible hand, Greenspan tied the visible hands of public officials who wanted to regulate financial markets, most egregiously in the case of Brooksley Born, the chair of the Commodity Futures Trading Commission in the late 1990s. Greenspan's successful campaign to undermine Born and prevent her from regulating the derivatives market led directly to the "subprime" crisis of 2008. During that crisis, before the House Committee on Oversight and Government Reform, Greenspan was finally made to confess his arrogance and folly: "Those of us who have looked to the self-interest of lending institutions to protect shareholders' equity, myself especially, are in a state of shock and disbelief."[19] As the chairman of the oversight committee, Representative Henry Waxman grilled Greenspan, the erstwhile Atlas of the free market himself now resembled a deflating bubble:

REP. WAXMAN: Well, where do you think you made a
    mistake, then?
MR. GREENSPAN: I made a mistake in presuming that the
    self-interest of organizations, specifically banks and others,
    were such as that they were best capable of protecting their
    own shareholders and their equity in the firms.

. . .

REP. WAXMAN: You had the authority to prevent irresponsible lending practices that led to the subprime mortgage crisis. You were advised to do so by many others. And now our whole economy is paying its price. Do you feel that your ideology pushed you to make decisions that you wish you had not made?

MR. GREENSPAN: Well, remember that what an ideology is, is a conceptual framework with the way people deal with reality. Everyone has one. You have to—to exist, you need an ideology. The question is whether it is accurate or not. And what I'm saying to you is, yes, I've found a flaw. I don't know how significant or permanent it is. But I've been very distressed by that fact.

. . .

REP. WAXMAN: You found a flaw in the reality . . .

MR. GREENSPAN: Flaw in the model that I perceived as the critical functioning structure that defines how the world works, so to speak.

REP. WAXMAN: In other words, you found that your view of the world, your ideology was not right. It was not working.

MR. GREENSPAN: Precisely. That's precisely the reason I was shocked, because I had been going for 40 years or more with very considerable evidence that it was working exceptionally well.[20]

Mother Jones' sardonic assessment of Greenspan's confession sums it up neatly: "In other words, whoops—there goes decades of Ayn Rand down the drain."[21]

Yves Smith (*nom de plume* of Susan Webber) effortlessly explains the flaw in Greenspan's "model": "Ideology-driven deregulation . . . shifted the investment banking world from a model driven by relationships with corporate clients to one in which making profits on every transaction was paramount."[22] The deregulation of the banking industry during the 1990s "changed businesses in which it had been easy to earn steady profits in conservative ways into businesses scrambling for profits, and as a consequence the industry gradually changed from a relatively low-risk 'fee-for-service' model to one where the big firms acted primarily as traders," and "traders tend to see transactions as a zero-sum game, even if the party on the other side is nominally a customer."[23] Competitive pressure in a vicious business environment has been a major factor in the transformation of banks into predator-speculators. "Idealizing the rational aspects of business decisions means refusing to notice behavior that is predatory, destructive, criminal, or simply stupid."[24] But refusing to notice that businessmen and bankers are sometimes motivated by misguided or fraudulent intentions is intellectually lazy and dishonest. Greenspan's economic paradigm "rests on assumptions that are patently ridiculous: that individuals are rational and utility-maximizing . . . that buyers and sellers have perfect information, that there are no transactions costs, that capitals flows freely."[25] Joseph Stiglitz explains this oversight in terms of so-called externalities:

Adam Smith, the father of modern economics, is often cited as arguing for the "invisible hand" and free markets: firms, in the pursuit of profits, are led, as if by an invisible hand, to do what is best for the world. But unlike his followers, Adam Smith was aware of some of the limitations of free markets, and research since then has further clarified why free markets, by themselves, often do not lead to what is best. . . . The reason that the invisible hand often seems invisible is that it is often not there. Whenever there are "externalities"—where the actions of an individual have impacts on others for which they do not pay, or for which they are not compensated— markets will not work well. Some of the important instances have long understood environmental externalities. Markets, by themselves, produce too much pollution. . . . But recent research has shown that these externalities are pervasive, whenever there is imperfect information or imperfect risk markets—that is always.[26]

Nouriel Roubini has pointed out that what Greenspan's "free market fundamentalist zealotry" lacked was common sense, an understanding "that market capitalism needs some basic and sensible rules, regulation and supervision to control excesses, bubbles, greed and investors' manias and panics."[27] Time and again, Greenspan foolishly counted on business to regulate itself, believing, in accordance with the simplistic logic of objectivism, that honest conduct is in the "self-interest" of any company that hopes to make money through a good reputation.

In the end the worship of "free markets" led to the rigging of all the markets: LIBOR, foreign exchange, gold, stocks—the scandals keep coming. This brings up another contradiction of objectivism: without suspecting it themselves, Greenspan and Rand were technocrats, and thus collectivists. To Chernyshevsky's (small) credit, he at least acknowledged his debt to Auguste Comte, one of the original inventors of technocracy, the belief in the necessity of rule by an elite panel of technical experts. As I show in Chapter 8, the Atlases of industry in Rand's novels are exemplary technocrats. When he first met Rand, Greenspan was "a talented technician, but that was all."[28] Rand reprogrammed him from "logical positivist" to "objectivist," but in the process only reinforced his sense that the world should be run by "technicians," which is to say by economic "forecasters," who worm their way into power in order that they might make their forecasts come true. One of the obvious implications of *Atlas Shrugged* is that the world should ideally belong to the technological innovators and technical experts. Naturally, the godlike arrogance of technocrats makes them blind to their shortcomings.

And so Greenspan's ignorance, dogmatism, and hubris blinded him to material proofs that invalidated his worldview. That is what you would expect from an ideologue. But now let us imagine a sociopath's encounter with objectivism, which tells him that his relentless, amoral pursuit of material or political gain is the very thing that makes him better than the people he tramples to get to the top. Presumably such a reader of Ayn Rand's novels does not probe deeply into this philosophy. He does not wince at Rand's stylistic lapses. Nor does he perform "due diligence" on the ideas presented. He plunders what he needs from them and goes back to work with the pleasant new belief that his rapaciousness has solid intellectual and even moral foundations. To some this justification of greed must be irresistible. Rand is still enormously popular, even in the wake of Greenspan's devastating activities. We are witnessing a surge of interest in Rand as a potential savior even in the face of the economic crisis that she helped to bring about. Thomas Frank has pointed out that the recent welfare payments to big banks resemble the sort of capital strike that John Galt arranged in *Atlas Shrugged*: "The bank bailouts and bonuses of 2008 and 2009 were done on an emergency basis, lest the geniuses of Wall Street shrug off their burden and abandon us to Great Depression II."[29] Former House Speaker John Boehner recently invoked the language of Ayn Rand, announcing that the nation's job creators were on strike.[30]

Hundreds of thousands of copies of *Atlas Shrugged* continue to sell every year: 500,000 copies in the crisis year of 2009 alone.[31] Three generations of entrepreneurs, corporate leaders, and politicians have grown up on Ayn Rand. Already in 1967 a young Ted Turner put up 248 billboards in the Southwest containing nothing but the famous question with which *Atlas Shrugged* begins, "Who is John Galt?". Mark Cuban, the owner of the Dallas Mavericks, and John P. Mackey, the chief executive of Whole Foods, have said that Ayn Rand helped them achieve business success.[32] In a 1966 letter Ronald Reagan called himself "an admirer of Ayn Rand." A 1987 article in *The New York Times* referred to her as the Reagan administration's "novelist laureate."[33] Senator Rand Paul, who claims he was not named after Ayn Rand, is, like his father, Ron Paul, a fan of her novels and thought.[34] Wisconsin senator Ron Johnson calls

Atlas Shrugged his "foundational book," and said in a 2010 debate that the novel is "a warning of what could happen to America." Each year, Justice Clarence Thomas hosts a screening of the 1949 film version of Rand's novel, *The Fountainhead*, for his new law clerks. Gary Johnson, the former New Mexico governor and Libertarian candidate for president, gave his fiancée a copy of *Atlas Shrugged* when they started dating, and told her, "If you want to understand me, read this."[35] In his essay for *Newsweek*, "Atlas Hugged," former South Carolina governor Mark Sanford confessed to having been "blown away" by Rand's novels in the eighties and in a baffling non sequitur declared that the 2008–09 financial crisis was the result of the free market being deprived of its "best minds."[36] At moments like this one grasps that objectivism, despite its name, is really a form of idealism that often crosses over into myth-making.

The inability to read literature goes hand in hand with an inability to read culture or even to know oneself. Understanding— whether of literature, culture, politics, economics, or self— requires hard work. Nabokov, in his parody of Chernyshevsky, was making two points: materialism is an inadequate worldview that did not even satisfy Chernyshevsky himself; forcing volatile ideological content into a faulty artistic form is a dangerous activity. Ayn Rand's favorite injunction, which occurs on the pages of *Atlas Shrugged*, and which she liked to fire at acquaintances and strangers alike, was "Check your premises!" I think her premises were wrong and that she acquired them secondhand. No wonder, then, that theft, whether in the form of plagiarism on the part of the authors or embezzlement on the part of the readers, has been a watermark of the financial crisis from the start. Theft, intellectual sloth, and opportunism are the legacy of Chernyshevsky and Rand.

Within the Trojan horse of Chernyshevsky's rational egoism lurked the image of his enigmatic revolutionary superman, Rakhmetov. As Russia's revolutionaries read *What Is to Be Done?* they took on board Rakhmetov's extremism, which they imitated and impersonated. This "Rakhmetovism" assumed two different forms: that of the suicide terrorist, known as the "mortus" (see Chapter 4), and that of the ruthless Jacobin dictator (see especially Chapter 6). Among the "mortuses" we can count Dmitry Karakozov, Nikolai Ishutin, and Sergei Nechaev (though Nechaev would have very much preferred to be a dictator). The principal Jacobin dictator was Lenin, but we also see this persona in Ayn Rand and "the Maestro," Alan Greenspan. Come to think of it, when "checking your premises," the first premise to check is that of selfhood: is it really you in there, or have you allowed yourself to become "the slave of some defunct economist," a "sleeper cell," the embodiment of a character in a novel? If it is you, it is probably safe to proceed to the next premise. If not, no logic can save you.

1

Radicalizing Dostoevsky

When seen in the light of Chernyshevsky, Dostoevsky's fiction falls into a clear pattern: before the encounter with Chernyshevsky, a series of interesting but fundamentally derivative works that here and there foreshadowed great things; after—strikingly original works of not unmarred genius. It was neither his exile to Siberia nor forced labor nor the death of his first wife nor his return to the capital cities that explains the change; no, it was precisely his reading of *What Is to Be Done?* that caused Dostoevsky's artistic renaissance. Chernyshevsky's ideology, particularly as presented in the novel, stoked up an inferno of disgust that tempered Dostoevsky's talent. At the same time the Chernyshevsky episode falls into a larger pattern in Dostoevsky's biography: a pendulum—or better, a Hegelian dialectic—that propelled him from reaction to revolution to reactionary revolution. In his youth in the 1840s, Dostoevsky had flirted with a radicalism as virulent as Chernyshevsky's in the 1860s. Dostoevsky's anti-nihilist novels of the 1860s and 1870s must have derived some of their reactionary vehemence from a desire on the part of a now loyal Dostoevsky to purge and punish the radical dissenter he had formerly been. In his angriest novel, *The Devils* (1872), *What Is to Be Done?* actually materializes in book form on a coffee table, propelling the plot into crisis. The anger Chernyshevsky's ideas stirred up in Dostoevsky helped him to discern what was laughable in the radicals and what he had to confront in a serious manner. In casting out the devils, though, Dostoevsky would have to start with himself.

He had grown up in the house of a religiously and politically conservative army doctor. His father doted on his children and taught them to love God and czar. Little Fedya (Fyodor) and his siblings feared their papa's displeasure, delighted him on his birthdays with recitations of French verse. At home they dutifully read Nikolai Karamzin's patriotic (propagandistic) *History of the Russian State* and the works of Russia's national poet, Alexander Pushkin. But sedition lurked below the placid surface. Pushkin had a naughty streak in him that colored his career. You see it, to give a few examples, in his sacrilegiously pornographic narrative poem "The Gabrieliad" (1821) (the poem is attributed to Pushkin based on strong evidence), in his biting epigrams, and in his youthful politics. Pushkin was exiled for reform-minded political activities in 1820. Upon his return to Russia in the mid-1820s he became friendly with the Decembrist rebels and wrote poems to the survivors of their ill-starred revolt of December 1825. Though Pushkin was implicated in the rebellion (his poems were found among the rebels' possessions), he was never charged with a crime. There is a story that Pushkin was setting out from his estate to St. Petersburg to join them when a hare (or possibly the village priest) crossed his path, causing him to cancel his plans and return home. One compelling interpretation of Pushkin's career is that while early in his life he flirted with radicalism in the form of libertinism and revolution, he repented after his return from exile, embracing more conservative religious, social, and political attitudes, returning, so to speak, to his native soil.[1] Dostoevsky, who idolized Pushkin and identified with him, would take comfort in the reflection that his life was following a similar path.

In the course of his studies at St. Petersburg's Engineering Institute in the late 1830s, Dostoevsky lost the three people who had influenced him the most: his mother and Pushkin in 1837 and then his father in 1839. He wrote that had he not been wearing mourning for his mother already, he would have worn black for Pushkin. The death of Dostoevsky's father was a murkier affair. Dr. Dostoevsky was murdered by his serfs, and Dostoevsky's preeminent biographer, Joseph Frank, has conjectured that the son's complicated feelings toward the father and toward the family serfs would likely have made him feel complicit in the murder. Dostoevsky loved the serfs and knew that they were human beings, who, as Karamzin had famously discovered, "also know how to love."[2] He had received breast milk and comfort from his family's house servants and had seen his parents' generous charity toward them when their village burned down. After the death of Dostoevsky's mother, his father had taken to drink and begun living with one of his housemaids, a young woman named Katerina. Whether he became neglectful or abusive toward his serfs during the last two years of his life is unknown. That would be a possible motivation for his murder. Another possibility is jealousy on the part of one or more of his serfs because of his affair with Katerina. A couple of poor harvests brought Dr. Dostoevsky and the whole village very close to rack and ruin, and Fyodor was exacerbating matters because he had failed to win a fellowship at the Engineering Academy and was constantly plaguing his father with requests for money. After the murder, Dostoevsky may have speculated that he had made a difficult situation worse, causing duress both to his father and to the peasants, and helping to bring things to crisis. If Dostoevsky suffered from a feeling that he was personally culpable for the hardships of a very specific group of peasants, then one can imagine that he felt authentic sympathy for the Russian peasantry as a whole. Within a decade he would risk freedom and life to plot their liberation.[3]

Learning that the czar was displeased by one of his military sketches, Dostoevsky resigned his commission and devoted himself to literature—a decision that already implies a degree of rebelliousness. The fact that Dostoevsky fell in first with Vissarion Belinsky and his radical literary circle falls into a pattern of protest in his earliest works. To set the stage, I will note that there was a line of literary descent from Pushkin to Gogol to Dostoevsky, and at the same time a power struggle playing out between authors and critics. As the aging poet Gavrila Derzhavin (1743–1816) had commended Russian literature into the hands of the young Pushkin, so Pushkin had blessed Nikolai Gogol, giving him the idea for his loftiest artistic achievements, his great play *The Inspector General* (1836) and tragicomic novel *The Dead Souls* (1842).[4] That apparently did not prevent Pushkin from misunderstanding Gogol's great work, for as Gogol read his novel aloud to Pushkin, Pushkin astonished him by exclaiming, "God, how sad our Russia is!" The great poet had misunderstood *The Dead Souls*; he had failed to notice that Gogol's mad lyricism had almost nothing to do with the real Russia.[5]

The most influential Russian critic of his age, Belinsky, also proved incapable of recognizing the nature of Gogol's genius. Belinksky attempted to find in Gogol's grotesqueries a flawless mirror of Russian reality and therefore an excoriation of serfdom and the czarist regime. "I loved you," Belinsky wrote to Gogol, "with all the passion with which a man, bound by ties of blood to his native country, can love its hope, its honor, its glory, one of its great leaders on the path toward consciousness, development, and progress."[6] But in a strange book titled *Select Passages from Correspondences with Friends* (1847) Gogol made it perfectly clear that he had written no such thing, that he was in fact a supporter of the existing order. This in turn provoked Belinsky to write one of the great flames of Russian literature, his open "Letter to Nikolai Gogol" (1847):

> One could endure an outraged sense of self-esteem, and I should have had sense enough to let the matter pass in silence were that the whole gist of it; but one cannot endure

an outraged sense of truth and human dignity; one cannot keep silent when lies and immorality are preached as truth and virtue under the guise of religion and the protection of the knout. . . . You failed to realize that Russia sees her salvation not in mysticism or asceticism or pietism, but in the successes of civilization, enlightenment, and humanity. What she needs is not sermons (she has heard enough of them!) or prayers (she has repeated them too often!), but the awakening in the people of a sense of their human dignity lost for so many centuries amid dirt and refuse; she needs rights and laws conforming not to the preaching of the church but to common sense and justice, and their strictest possible observance. . . . Proponent of the knout, apostle of ignorance, champion of obscurantism and Stygian darkness, panegyrist of Tartar morals—what are you about. Look beneath your feet—you are standing on the brink of an abyss![7]

Passing over the parenthetical question of whether or not Belinsky's appraisal of Gogol's political and religious intelligence hits close to the mark (I think it does), we can say for certain that it was Belinsky's own fault that he bungled his reading of *The Dead Souls*. Not until much later did literary criticism begin to recognize Gogol's novel for what it is: a poetic, emotional, dazzling performance that has very little to do with social morals or even social reality. Gogol recanted, left the fray, became religious, and soon died of self-inflicted inanition. Belinsky was painfully disappointed by the "apostasy" of Gogol, but his relentless calls for a new "Natural School" of literature inspired a generation of young writers to try their hands at "physiologies"—unflinchingly realistic sketches of the injustices of Russian reality. Dostoevsky's first novel, *Poor Folk* (1845), was much closer to what Belinsky had in mind. This is no surprise, given that it was made to order.

A far better reader than Belinsky, Dostoevsky did in fact grasp the quirky genius of Gogol, but that did not prevent him from creating in *Poor Folk* a sentimental and derivative work in which Belinsky could recognize just the sort of "social novel" that he had been calling for. The critic—this time correctly— found in the mawkish *Poor Folk* an expression of "humanistic" pity for the downtrodden. Unlike Gogol's human insects, Dostoevsky's wretches have an unconquerable dignity and, implicitly, "rights." Two other budding young authors, Dmitry Grigorovich and Nikolai Nekrasov, read the manuscript of *Poor Folks* aloud through the night with tears in their eyes, and, the next day, brought it to Belinsky. Belinsky's praise for *Poor Folks* may be seen as a sort of radical blessing upon Dostoevsky's literary career. At first Belinsky boasted of his great find in a paternalistic, patronizing tone, but this praise was hastily bestowed, hastily withdrawn. Dostoevsky's early success went directly to his head, which was part of the reason he did not get along with Belinsky and his entourage. Turgenev, in particular, found a wicked pleasure in baiting Dostoevsky, forcing him to take up indefensible positions in arguments and then watching as Dostoevsky tried to defend them, blushing, spluttering, and thrashing in the net. Nekrasov and his friend Ivan Panaev got to work satirizing Dostoevsky's social ineptitude in a suite of evil stories and poems. Beyond this bad chemistry, there was a substantive reason for the schism. Dostoevsky had argued with Belinsky about the function of art, insisting that "art has no necessity to have a tendency, that art is an end in itself, that an author should concern himself only with artistic quality and the idea will come by itself."[8] The one thing that Belinsky demanded of artists, however, was the pursuit of political and social ideas of a particular tendency. It is interesting to see the young Dostoevsky state so strongly that artistic considerations must come first for an artist, because, as I will show, he was ever at war with himself over this very point in his finest novels.

The consumptive Belinsky did not have long to live, and the criticism he wrote in his final year or two anticipates Chernyshevsky, who was to take up the blood-spattered mantle of Russia's literary conscience less than a decade later. Belinsky deplored Dostoevsky's post-*Poor-Folk* novellas—*The Double* and *The Landlady*—because they were written in a fantastical, neo-gothic style that provoked Belinsky's new mood of virulent antipathy to anything but "critical" realism. Belinsky had by now rejected the idealism of his youth and wanted political reform. Art's purpose was to make this program perfectly clear and give it a sense of urgency. Appeals to Christian charity or humanism were pointless; now Belinsky was drawn more and more to reason as the only engine of progressive humanity. Belinsky had read Max Stirner's *The Ego and His Own* (1845), and in 1847 he told his friend Annenkov that people could be brought beyond Stirner's brand of egoism to the realization that their "egotistical interests are identical with that of mankind as a whole."[9] It is worth noting that Belinsky twisted Stirner's philosophy of uncompromising individualism, perverting it into its very antithesis: collectivism. The idea I want to express here is that in the final years of his life Belinsky sketched out the ideological system that Chernyshevsky would soon after put to canvas in garish detail. The prime value of the system was equality; the method was reason; the motivation—egoism. Art was supposed to use the method to indicate the value.

Falling out with Belinsky and his circle, Dostoevsky began, in 1847, attending evenings at the house of Mikhail Butashevich-Petrashevsky. Petrashevsky was an eccentric nobleman and self-professed socialist who dabbled in the thinking of Charles Fourier and Ludwig Feuerbach. What attracted Petrashevsky to Fourier was the idea of the phalanstery as the ideal organizing structure of society. The phalanstery—a form of communal housing, and indeed an architectural structure that Fourier drafted in minute detail—was, fantastically, supposed to heal the rifts that fragmented society, bringing urban and rural into balance, harmonizing men and women, and transforming labor into a joyful and fulfilling activity. Humans were to redefine their relationship with nature, cultivate an intensely sensual life, and perfect themselves through self-realization. Petrashevsky believed that the phalanstery would eventually usher in a socialist utopia to replace the misery and injustice that reigned. The other main source of ideas for Petrashevsky was the anthropotheist philosophy of Feuerbach. Feuerbach described the need for "the substitution of the human for the divine being" and wanted to raise "anthropology to the rank of theology."[10] He understood Christianity to have been a step in the right direction, for it synthesized God and Man into the God-Man—in other words, the God who became a man, that is, Christ. What was now needed was a further step to bring about the Man-God. The Petrashevskyite Dmitry Akhsharumov gave a speech in honor of Fourier, which exemplifies the slipshod manner in which Petrashevsky and his circle fused Fourier and Feuerbach, idealism and naturalism:

> We ought to remember what a great task we have undertaken: to restore the laws of nature trampled underfoot by ignorance, to reinstate the divine aspect of man in all its greatness, to liberate and organize his lofty and harmonious passions, which have been cured and inhibited. To tear down towns and capital cities; to use their bricks and mortar to erect other buildings; to transform a life full of pain, unhappiness, poverty, shame, and humiliation into a life full of splendor, harmony, joy, wealth, and happiness; to cover the face of the earth with palaces and fruits; to adorn it with flowers— behold, that is our goal, our great goal, the greatest of all goals that the earth has ever known.[11]

Chernyshevsky would later assimilate from the Petrashevsky crowd this jumble of Fourier and Feuerbach.

The members of the circle met on Fridays to read forbidden books and articles and to discuss their socialist dreams and theories. In early 1848 Dostoevsky attended Fridays at Petrashevsky's infrequently and described them with derision as the frivolous and self-indulgent pastime of people who liked to "play at liberalism."[12] All of the theoretical talk and socialist utopianism repulsed Dostoevsky, who told an acquaintance that a phalanstery must be worse than any prison.[13] Dostoevsky maintained that Russians

> should seek for the sources of a development of Russian society not in the doctrines of Western Socialists, but in the life and age-old historical organization of [the Russian] people, where in the *obshchina* [communal ownership of land] and *artel* [worker's wage-sharing cooperative], and in the principles of mutual village responsibility [for the payment of taxes], there have long since existed much more solid and normal foundations.[14]

We see in this attitude an early intimation of Dostoevsky's "Russian Idea" of the 1860s rather than a voguish adherence to French and German imported models of socialism. Still, the Petrashevsky Circle was destined to play a tumultuous role in Dostoevsky's life, for it was here that he met his "personal Mephistopheles," Nikolai Speshnev, and Speshnev drew Dostoevsky straight into a form of revolutionary radicalism that was anything but liberal posturing.

Lenin wrote that the history of the socialist intelligentsia in Russia began with the Petrashevsky Circle.[15] It is unknown how much Lenin had discovered about Speshnev, but, unlike Petrashevsky, Speshnev was in fact just the sort of man Lenin most esteemed: rationally calculating, philosophically enlightened, politically uncompromising, and prepared for action. In his own words Speshnev was "such an inveterate atheist and materialist of the school of Dézamy that the very word 'spirit' brings an evil sneer to [his] lips, a man who not only believes in no symbol of faith . . . but believes in nothing at all and recognizes only what he sees, hears or reaches by the path of logical deduction."[16] Speshnev had studied at the Lycée with Petrashevsky and left Russia in 1842 to live in Paris. There he moved in revolutionary circles. He was also very close to the Polish revolutionary movement. Upon his return in 1846, he introduced revolutionary communism into Russia. His wanted to combine the social utopia of Fourier and the communism of Theodore Dézamy into what he described as "a social system which will transform self-interest into solidarity, social interest, where all men will work because they want to, not just to get paid." Production, wrote Speshnev, "will be regulated by the great principles of Fourier and consumption by the general communist principle of equal distribution."[17]

To attain this idea, Speshnev intended to start a revolution and overthrow the czarist regime. His methods were those of the French Jacobins. Speshnev was very well versed in the history and methods of secret societies. He had read the Jesuit Abbé Barruel's *Mémoires pour server à l'histoire du Jacobinisme*, Buanarroti's *Conspiration pour l'égalité dite de Babeuf*, Eugène Sue's *Le Juif errant*, and Dézamy's *Le Jésuitisme vaincu et anéanti par le socialism* (which was in his possession at the time of his arrest). He had also observed the running of secret societies in Europe firsthand.[18] Though he later had to destroy it, he had even written a book on the subject, ending it with a chapter on the best way of establishing a secret revolutionary society in Russia.[19] He favored Dézamy's methods, the ruthless seizure of power and suppression of resistance through terror, over the more peaceful systems of socialist utopians like Etienne Cabet.[20] In particular he was partial to the ancient conspiratorial technique of rings within rings: an inner circle with a secret purpose of its own recruits from a larger outer circle, which often has no knowledge of the plans or even existence of the inner circle.[21] Speshnev's conception of an inner ring of dedicated communists drew upon the principles of the Jesuits, which he knew from Dézamy, upon Nicholas Bonneville, and upon the Illuminists. With these tools in hand, Speshnev trawled the Petrashevsky Circle for men who were willing to go beyond merely dabbling at socialism.

At Petrashevsky's Speshnev vied with Petrashevsky himself for dominance, and the two clashed several times over the matter of method. Relying on his good looks, charisma, and eloquence, Speshnev carefully constructed a cult of personality. He maintained an enigmatic silence most of the time, but now and then dropped hints about his revolutionary struggles and love affairs in Europe. He also spread the canard that he was an agent of an international revolutionary conspiracy. By these means he won over the support of many Petrashevskyites, although Petrashevsky himself did not believe him.[22] Speshnev argued for the use of terror and presented a program of infiltration (Jesuitism), propaganda, and revolt.[23] In a document that was found among Speshnev's possessions upon his arrest, the only surviving fragment of his book on secret societies, he proposed to forge a group of conspirators, binding them with the following oath:

> When the Executive Committee of the Society, after assessing the powers of the Society, abiding conditions and suitable circumstance, decides that it is time to revolt, I promise, with no attempt to spare myself, to take full and open part in the insurrection and fight. That is, upon notification by the Committee, I promise to appear at the appointed day, hour and place and to appear there and once there, taking up firearm or cold steel or both, not sparing myself, to take part in the fight and by any means available to me to facilitate the success of the insurrection.[24]

Speshnev plotted to create a Russian society, a network of circles, with five conspirators per circle. Each conspirator had to promise to recruit five more, each of whom would sign the same oath. When Petrashevsky opposed Speshnev's program of action, arguing that revolution must ripen organically over time in the minds of the peasants, Speshnev became impatient and went ahead on his own, forging his own secret radical ring within the larger Petrashevsky group.[25]

It was when Dostoevsky, always hard up for money, accepted a loan from Speshnev that he told his friend, Dr. Yanovsky, about this arrangement and its metaphysical consequences:

> I have taken money from Speshnev (he named a sum of about five hundred rubles) and now I am *with him* and *his*. I'll never be able to pay back such a sum, yes, and he wouldn't take the

money back; that's the kind of man he is. . . . Do you understand, from now on I have a Mephistopheles of my own![26]

It is not known whether Speshnev had forced Dostoevsky to sign the promissory note cited above when he handed him the loan, but he somehow managed to recruit Dostoevsky into his first revolutionary cell. What jumps out at this point in the story is the paradox that in attempting to liberate the serfs, Dostoevsky had compromised *himself*, even to the point of enslavement.

This became irrelevant on April 22, 1849, when Petrashevsky and the frequenters of his salon, Dostoevsky and Speshnev included, were arrested for sedition and then sentenced to death by firing squad. Dostoevsky was so psychologically crushed by his obligations to Speshnev that he positively rejoiced at this calamity: "I would have lost my mind if not for the catastrophe [the arrest] that broke my life. An idea had appeared before which my health and worries turned out to be trifles."[27] The main charge against Dostoevsky was that he had read Belinsky's "Letter to Gogol" aloud at one of Petrashevsky's gatherings. Eight months later, in late December of the same year, the Petrashevskyites were taken to St. Petersburg's Semenovsky Square and grouped in trios. Dostoevsky had minutes left to live. Awaiting his turn, staring at the rising sun, in a state of great excitement, he had the following characteristic exchange with Speshnev. "Nous serons avec le Christ," said Dostoevsky, completely forgetting his revolutionary atheism. His personal Mephistopheles, who was made of more solid material (from a communist point of view), retorted, "Un peu de poussière."[28] Here again is evidence that

Dostoevsky was unable to shake off his Christian upbringing and was thus fundamentally out of place among the socialists. At this fraught moment, a messenger from the czar came galloping and conveyed to the prisoners that their lives had been spared, their sentences commuted to hard labor followed by exile. Dostoevsky's new sentence was four years of hard labor and another six years of exile from the capital cities.

Dostoevsky rejoiced, writing to his brother that very day, describing himself as reborn. He had wasted too much precious time before and now swore to cherish his life and devote it to better things. The only book prisoners like Dostoevsky were allowed to read during their Siberian captivity was the New Testament. The Dostoevsky who returned to St. Petersburg ten years later was much changed from the reluctant revolutionist of the late forties. He knew what it was to be a revolutionary and what it was to return repentant to Christianity. He had met the devil himself in the person of the extremist Speshnev, and he would nurse the image of the revolutionary superman in his imagination until he had discovered an aesthetic form suitable for its deployment. The idea of the superman was first seen, tentatively, in *Crime and Punishment*, then decisively in *The Devils*.

But Dostoevsky was not the only one to be so captivated by Speshnev. We see in Speshnev the outline of Chernyshevsky's rational egoism and of his socialist utopia. We also see in him a possible historical prototype for his uncompromising revolutionary superman, the "rigorist" Rakhmetov. Chernyshevsky's followers, Nikolai Ishutin, Dmitry Karakozov, Pyotr Tkachev,

Sergei Nechaev, Alexander Ulyanov, and his younger brother Vladimir (Lenin), would all employ the Jacobinian means championed by Speshnev in pursuit of their revolutionary ends, but the "person" they were most clearly trying to incarnate was Rakhmetov. While Speshnev never returned from his Siberian exile, word of him and his ideas did escape back to the capital cities. At least some of these revolutionaries knew of him. A haze of rumors and legends descended on the scene. Literature became contaminated by history and history by literature, and it reached the point where it was hard to judge whether a given revolutionary was imitating Speshnev or Rakhmetov or both. This cross-contamination between reality and fiction was in fact Chernyshevsky's purpose in creating "the most atrocious work of Russian literature."

2

"The most atrocious work of Russian literature"

I do not possess a shred of artistic talent. In fact my command of the language is poor. But never mind: read on, my indulgent audience! It will not be a total waste of your time. Truth is a fine thing: it compensates for the shortcomings of the writer who serves it. I will therefore tell you: if I had not warned you, it would perhaps have seemed to you that my novel was artistically written, that the author possesses much lyrical talent. But I did warn you that I have no talent. You will therefore know that all the virtues of this novel derive only from its truthfulness.

NIKOLAI CHERNYSHEVSKY, *WHAT IS TO BE DONE?*[1]

Chernyshevsky's famous novel was initially received with astonished disgust by the Russian intelligentsia. One critic called *What Is to Be Done?* "the most atrocious work of Russian literature."[2] Alexander Herzen, the very soul and conscience of reform-minded progressives in Russia, read Chernyshevsky's *What Is to Be Done?* in 1867 in his London exile, four years after the book's publication and described his impressions in a letter to the poet and radical Nikolai Ogarev, also in European exile: "I am reading Chernyshevskii's novel. Good Lord, how basely it is written, how much affectation . . . what style! What a worthless generation whose aesthetics are satisfied by this."[3] Ivan Turgenev, to whose novel *Fathers and Children* Chernyshevsky's *opus* was a direct response, complained to the great poet Afanasy Fet that he was "swallowing [Chernyshevsky's] style with the greatest difficulty."[4] Upon finishing the book, Turgenev wrote that Chernyshevsky's "manner arouses physical disgust in me, like wormseed. . . . I had never met an author whose figures stank. . . . Chernyshevskii unwittingly appears to me a naked and toothless old man who lisps like an infant."[5] Fet marveled at "the cynical silliness of the whole novel" and at "the obvious collusion of the censorship."[6]

How indeed could a police state allow the publication—twice—of a work that instantly created a role model for so many terrorists? Lenin praised *What Is to Be Done?* above all other books precisely because "hundreds of people became revolutionaries under its influence."[7] If the novel was so effective at radicalizing young people, how strange that the censors passed it. Several theories have been proposed to explain this. One is that the censors did not read the novel carefully. Another is that the czar's head censor, V. N. Beketov, who liked to flaunt his liberalism, strove to maintain a facade of good relations with the liberals of Nekrasov and Chernyshevsky's set. A third explanation claims that Chernyshevsky disguised the novel's message so well that he fooled the censors (but not the reading public). I am persuaded by Andrew Drozd's argument that the censorship hoped Chernyshevsky's quasi-literate style would turn the novel into an embarrassment for the revolutionary cause.[8] Nabokov argues the same in *The Gift*: "The censorship permitted it to be published in *The Contemporary*, reckoning . . . that a novel which was 'something in the highest degree anti-artistic' would be certain to overthrow Chernyshevski's authority, that he would simply be laughed at for it."[9] Instead, published first serially and then as a book, it was received as the revolutionary's user manual. The government finally sprang into action, banning it and attempting to scrounge up all the infected issues of *The Contemporary*. Looking for someone to blame, the Third Department (secret police) blamed the censor, and the censor blamed the Third Department, to no avail.

To understand the novel's conceptual origins, we must return a few years in time and examine Chernyshevsky's formative reading material. During the seventeenth and eighteenth centuries, the European Enlightenment had favored reason and scientific method, putting man at the center of a rational universe. In the mid-nineteenth century, a resurgent Enlightenment adopted new trends of thought: materialism, positivism, utilitarianism, and socialism. Chernyshevsky's main sources were Ludwig Feuerbach, Ludwig Büchner, Auguste Comte, Charles Fourier, and Max Stirner. Following his materialist teachers (Feuerbach,

Büchner), Chernyshevsky disavowed the dualism of corporeal and spiritual, declaring an absolute materialist monism. True, it is not a monism that holds up on a close reading of the novel, but Chernyshevsky thought he was being consistent. Mind and spirit were supposed to be one with body, all part of nature. To understand any part of nature, including emotion, thought, desire, one needed to cast aside dangerous superstitions like religion and philosophical idealism, and turn to science. Comte conceived of sociology as the science of sciences, the ultimate boon of reason. When properly understood, humanity might be perfectible. Reaching a "scientific" understanding of society, people must overthrow the beneficiaries of a false and defunct worldview: monarchy, aristocracy, and church.

The extent of Chernyshevsky's revolutionary activities is still debated. In 1861 the radicals rallied around his journal, *The Contemporary*, and were conspiring with their counterparties at Herzen's London-based journal, *The Bell*.[10] They created a new great revolutionary society: the Land and Freedom party. Its name came from a sentence in a manifesto that Herzen had coauthored with Ogarev: "What the people need is land and freedom." The organizational structure was the very same as in Nikolai Speshnev's system: a network of five-man cells that grows exponentially as each cell member recruits four new members; each conspirator knows the four members of the cell into which he was recruited plus the four new members he recruits.[11] Some historians speculate that Chernyshevsky was a member of Land and Freedom from its founding, while others hold that despite his agreement with the principles of the movement, he felt constrained, being under surveillance, to limit his activities to his work for *The Contemporary*.[12] Whichever the case, Chernyshevsky was recognized as Land and Freedom's inspiration.

Since the revolutionary movement in Russia began with the Decembrist Revolt of 1825 and the Petrashevsky Circle of the 1840s, Nikolai Speshnev was a probable inspiration for Chernyshevsky, whose character Rakhmetov seems partly based on that strong-willed aristocrat who gave up wealth and prestige to serve the downtrodden. The milder Petrashevskyites were also appealing to Chernyshevsky. This included Petrashevsky himself, who had introduced the radical Russian intelligentsia to Fourier and Feuerbach. Fourier's phalanstery becomes Chernyshevsky's palace of aluminum and glass, the dream vision of a utopian socialist future in *What Is to Be Done?* And Feuerbach's anthropotheism comes to life in the novel's main characters, the revolutionary superman Rakhmetov and socialist superwoman Vera Pavlovna. A strange duality arises here in Russian thought, later to persist into the Soviet period. You might call the phenomenon "Waiting for Rakhmetov." Chernyshevsky insisted that the artist must never depict reality as transcendent. Art must imitate reality, but only that part of reality which exemplifies a progression from the human present to the superhuman (socialist) future: in other words, only the transcendent part of reality! The main heirs of Chernyshevsky's bumbling, illogical aesthetic were the Soviet-mandated novels of socialist realism and the "capitalist realism" of Ayn Rand. In these works Feuerbachian man-gods or supermen overturn a foul existing order through revolutionary discipline, preparing the advent of the sacred future of socialism. Or indeed capitalism— the choice appears to be arbitrary.

In the spirit of Comte, Chernyshevsky wanted literature to observe reality with "scientific" objectivity, criticizing its shortcomings and offering up improvements. Already in his master's thesis of 1855 Chernyshevsky insisted that scientific rigor be applied to aesthetics: "Respect for the reality of life, mistrust for *a priori* hypotheses, as pleasant as they may be to our fancy—such is the trend that now reigns in science. . . . It is essential to use this common denominator in discussing our aesthetic convictions as well."[13] Chernyshevsky is explicitly reacting against Hegelian aesthetics, which defined the beautiful as (in Chernyshevsky's paraphrase) "the perfect correlation, the perfect identity of idea and image" or "the full manifestation of an idea in a given object."[14] To Chernyshevsky—in theory—this was all rubbish and superstition. A work of art was bad to the extent that it dreamed of an ideal world or an alternative to reality. It was good only inasmuch as it was useful; it was useful only inasmuch as it promoted improvements upon reality. Improvements were to be understood as changes that were progressive, better yet revolutionary, best of all socialistic. Turgenev described Chernyshevsky's master's thesis as "a rotten corpse . . . the result of malicious stupidity."[15] "With their insolence," he wrote, "they want to wipe from the face of the earth poetry, the fine arts, all aesthetic pleasures and introduce their own coarse seminarist principles. They are literary Robespierres."[16] Fair enough, but I want to point out the contradiction between Chernyshevsky's aesthetic principles and practice. What is Chernyshevsky's technique in *What Is to Be Done?* if not "the perfect correlation of idea and image," where the idea is revolution and the image Rakhmetov? How are imagined "improvements" upon the status quo different from fantasies about "an alternative to reality"? When judged by the criteria of his own master's thesis, Chernyshevsky's novel is a fail.

Chernyshevsky's theory of art is wound up and set madly spinning in his novel. *What Is to Be Done?* presents the reader with the predicament of Vera Rozalsky, a young lady who lives as a virtual slave to her parents in 1850s St. Petersburg. Her tyrannical mother wants to marry her off to a debauched officer whose father owns the tenement block where they live. A medical student named Dmitry Lopukhov intervenes to save her. Lopukhov has been frequenting the Rozalsky home as the tutor of Vera's little brother. They discuss socialist books and ideas of justice. Lopukhov contrives to marry Vera before her unwanted suitor can, and the two move to their own apartment, living together as friends, in separate bedrooms, with an elaborate set of rules to guarantee their privacy, freedom, and equality. To gain her financial independence from Lopukhov, Vera joins up with other young women and establishes a communal sewing business. The seamstresses live together and share the profits. Because the interest of each seamstress coincides with the interests of the collective, the business is successful. Vera is not attracted to Lopukhov and falls in love with his best friend and classmate Alexander Kirsanov, who is, like Lopukhov, a socialist. Lopukhov decides to remove himself from this frustrating equation by faking his suicide and relocating to America. He is assisted by an extraordinary person named Rakhmetov, who has previously been radicalized by Kirsanov. Rakhmetov brings the grieving Vera a note from Lopukhov. The ruse is explained. Lopukhov's exit clears the way for Vera and Kirsanov, who eventually marry. Meanwhile Lopukhov, under the pseudonym of Charles Beaumont, makes his fortune in America, secretly returns to Russia, and marries an industrialist's daughter, Katherine Polozova, whom Kirsanov had saved from a wasting disease. The "Beaumonts" and Kirsanovs live together in a kind of *ménage a quatre*. The sewing commune is rapidly expanding. Vera gives it all up in order to study medicine, the preferred profession of nineteenth-century Russian socialists.

The book's style is a jarring cacophony of disparate elements. A coy and patronizing narrator constantly intrudes into the action in a tone at once bumbling and superior. The Russian poet Afanasy Fet criticized Chernyshevsky for "premeditated affectation of the worst sort in terms of form and that totally helpless clumsiness of language," which "make the reading of the novel a difficult, almost unbearable, task."[17] Through constant asides, Chernyshevsky derides us for not understanding the rituals and private jokes of the "new" progressives. To the image of a socialist created by Marx and Fourier, Chernyshevsky adds his own special brand: rational egoism. Kirsanov, Lopukhov, Rakhmetov, and Vera live according to enlightened self-interest. Whenever one of them appears to do something irrational or, worse, philanthropical, he panics and rushes to find some way to square his action with rational egoism. Then the narrator, too, leaps to his character's defense with many winks and strained jokes. This constant ideological hedging becomes a second characteristic component of the novel's tone. The third: a creepy sexual tension, which sees Lopukhov lust after Vera, Vera rejecting his advances, yet teasing him with chaste little kisses and even allowing him, in place of a handmaid, to help dress her. Chernyshevsky maintains this embarrassing tension through half the book. A fourth element of the novel's style is the exasperating tedium of socialist sermonizing by the narrator and his socialist heroes. Then there is the escalating awkwardness of four fantastic "revolutionary" dreams that Vera has over the course of the novel. Infamous in Russian literature, these dreams occur within their own separate sections of the novel titled accordingly—"Vera Pavlovna's First Dream," "Vera Pavolovna's Second Dream," etc.—each presided over by an allegorical feminine figure representing Love or Equality, an idealized version of Vera herself. Although ludicrous, these dreams merit our attention for their subversive role in Chernyshevsky's novel aesthetics.

Vera Pavlovna's first dream

In Vera's dreams Chernyshevsky's materialist enthusiasm takes on a religious dimension. Her first dream occurs after she and Lopukhov have agreed to set her up as governess in the house of an acquaintance and thus put an end to Vera's sufferings in her parents' home. Vera's dream-self, stricken with "paralysis," is "locked in a wet, dark basement" when "suddenly the door opened, and Verochka [i.e. Vera] found herself in a field; she runs around, she romps and thinks, 'How on earth did I manage not to die in that basement? It is because I had not yet seen this field. Had I seen it, I would have died in the basement.'" Next the dream goddess appears, telling Vera to call her "Love for the People." It was she who released Vera from the basement. Vera then goes through town letting other young women out of basements and curing their paralysis, so they can "romp" as well.[18]

In Book Seven of Plato's *Republic*, the character Socrates describes a prisoner trapped in an underground cave and tied up so that he must always face a wall. Behind the prisoner burns a fire, and his jailors pass objects before the fire so that shadows play on the wall. The shadows are the prisoner's sole reality until he is freed from his chains and contemplates the fire and puppets. When he is subsequently dragged out from the cave into the world outside, he grasps a deeper reality. Such a prisoner, explains Socrates, will not willingly return to the cave or accept shadows as reality. By employing Plato's metaphor, Chernyshevsky suggests that Vera must escape her mother's house, grow in her understanding of the world and in the role she is to play in it.

Vera's governess position falls through. In despair, she begins to compare various methods of suicide, eventually plumping for asphyxiation. Lopukhov has a better idea: he sneaks into Vera's room and proposes that they marry fictitiously and live together on a chaste, comradely basis. Since her mother would never allow

Vera to marry a poor student, elopement is the only way. Right then and there, rules for fair communal living are cheerfully established. They agree to elope once Lopukhov finishes medical school and begins working as a doctor. Returning home that evening, Lopukhov reflects on his arrangement with Vera. The narrator comments that this is natural for a materialist like Lopukhov who "only ever thinks about what is in his own best interest. And he truly was thinking about what was in his own best interest. Instead of lofty poetic and Platonic daydreams, he was occupied with the sort of romantic daydreams that are appropriate to a crude materialist."[19] The uncomprehending mention of "Platonic daydreams" is symptomatic. What Lopukhov is fretting over is that Vera is bound to decide sooner or later that he has sacrificed himself for her, giving up a brilliant career in medicine. In an absurd interior monolog, Lopukhov tries to convince himself that he remains a good rational egoist although he has embarked upon the path of philanthropy, the very antithesis of rational egoism. He repeats over and over again that since he loves Vera he is not sacrificing himself for her but pursuing self-interest. While presented as the basis of rational egoism, logic is contrived and unstable in this novel. If we understand "love" as a state in which one desires another's happiness more than one's own, then Chernyshevsky's whole fragile system of rational egoism goes to pieces.

A worse lapse of logic occurs when Lopukhov declares that it was he himself, not Vera, whom he released from that "basement." How can he know about her basement dream in the first place, if she never told him? Verisimilitude is not one of this novel's strengths, but this porous quality of Vera's dreams is intentional. Chernyshevsky uses Plato's story of the cave to attack the sociopolitical order of his day. The czar, the church, and their minions are the "cave" or "basement." Socialism is the world above ground, under the sun. The philosopher must throw off deceptions as he passes through the delusions of the world of objects and approaches perfection in the world of forms. Does this scheme not contradict Chernyshevsky's materialist worldview? It does, and blatantly. What Chernyshevsky probably found most tempting in *The Republic* was the image of utopia as a collective ruled over by a philosopher king, managed by a political elite that Plato called "guardians." Chernyshevsky's "new people," the revolutionary avant-garde, are his guardians.

Vera Pavlovna's second dream

The old couple who lease an apartment to the Lopukhovs quaintly decide that Vera and Dmitry must belong to a sect, since they never seem to make love but instead observe all manner of formality regarding privacy, knocking before entering, receiving one another in formal attire. The narrator is smirking a bit at the landlords' backwardness, but, truth be told, Vera and Lopukhov do belong to a sect—a socialist utopian order. At their apartment the Lopukhovs frequently receive guests, with whom, over dinner, they discuss the pressing matters of the day: "the chemical rudiments of agriculture," "the laws of historical progress," and "the great importance of distinguishing real desires from fantastical ones."[20] These "new people" apply their "scientific method" to everything and everyone. It goes without saying that their "science" is almost entirely fantasy. The "laws" of historical progress are the speculative theories of Hegel and possibly Marx. They attach "great importance" to rejecting certain desires as false and fantastical while retaining others as authentic, because Chernyshevsky's rational egoism requires people to act on their desires, but only those desires that are underwritten by logic, and only that logic which leads to socialism.

These silly conversations beget Vera's "Second Dream," in which Lopukhov and a friend tediously discuss the chemical properties of soil. Agriculture serves here as a metaphor for revolution. There are two types of soil. One, which allegorically represents the current state of the Russian people, is described as rancid, foul-smelling, "fantastical", and stagnant due to a lack of drainage. This is the swampy terrain of Christianity, all clogged up with fantastical notions like charity and the other world. The second soil is healthy and "real," because workers have installed a drainage system. Work creates movement, and movement defines life: "for work is, according to anthropological analysis, the form of movement, which supplies the basis for all the other forms: recreation, relaxation, entertainment, merriment; without work, they have no reality."[21] Water, the reader must understand, moves through irrigated soil like socialism through the mind of a people. Work and recreation will become the basic features of Vera's utopian vision in her fourth dream.

Vera's dreams exist so that the "new people" may smuggle ideological contraband out of them into reality. What Vera takes from her second dream is the concept that work must form the basis of life. Waking, she immediately busies herself with her sewing cooperative. Once the rules of communal labor and profit-sharing have been articulated, the seamstresses take their families, friends, and suitors on a weekend boat excursion. Enter Chernyshevsky's as yet unnamed revolutionary superhero, Rakhmetov. During the outing Lopukhov vies with two students in a strange test of the purity of their socialist thinking. One of the students is identified, based on his brand of socialism, as "the Romantic" and the other as "the Rigorist." Lopukhov's position makes him "the Schematic." Only much later—in Vera's third dream—do we learn that the "Rigorist" is Rakhmetov. By the end of the argument, Lopukhov has evolved into an "Auguste-Comtian," and a young officer arrives to replace Lopukhov as the "Schematist."[22] As proof of his logical "rigor," Rakhmetov proceeds to beat up Lopukhov—and also the young officer-Schematist, whose sole function in the novel is to be beaten up. The young socialists let brute force decide whose socialism is best. Revolution necessitates violence, so the "rigorous" revolutionary keeps his body strong, ready for battle.

Events now build toward the crisis. Lopukhov catches a cold during his fisticuffs. Kirsanov, who comes to treat Lopukhov at Vera's request, ends up staying a couple of nights, affording Vera the opportunity to fall in love with him. The narrator shirks the task of describing Kirsanov, claiming that he has already done so by describing Lopukhov, for they are as similar as two cogs in a clockwork. The narrator explains that though there are some superficial differences between the two friends—Lopukhov learns

French by reading François Fénelon's *Adventures of Telemachus, Son of Ulysses* (1699), while Kirsanov reads the New Testament in French nine times in a row[23]—these negligible variations only serve to indicate the profound underlying similarity. They are two robots made in the same factory. The narrator concludes his comparison of the two by asking, "How on earth can you tell such people apart? All of their most sharply defined traits are those not of individuals but of a type." The people who make up this "type" are all brave, practical, reliable, strong, unwavering, and "impeccably honest."[24] The narrator prophesies that this new type of Russian will be called upon by the masses to lead a revolution; then they will be hissed at, shamed, and driven away; next they will be remembered and missed; finally, "this type will cease to exist separately, because all people will be of this type."[25] In brief, an inferno of impeccably honest robots.

There is, nonetheless, one difference between the two cogs that is important to the plot: Vera is sexually attracted to her husband's friend, but not to her husband. Unable to cast off his role of family doctor, Kirsanov diagnoses Vera and finds that she is in love with him but does not yet know it. Upon Lopukhov's recovery, Kirsanov faces a dilemma. To have an affair with Vera would be "to destroy the peace of mind of a woman whose life is going well." Yet it "is too late to fix this situation by running away. I don't know how it will play out, but fleeing or remaining are equally dangerous to you, and for the people whose peace of mind you are trying to preserve, your flight would perhaps be even more perilous than remaining."[26] Another rational egoist caught in the act of selflessly worrying about others.

Chernyshevsky hastens to stomp out this contradiction. Kirsanov now tries to find some personal gain that will obscure the too-obvious fact that he has been unselfishly worrying about preserving the familial harmony of his friends. There is no God and no charity among rational adults. What is there then? Well, this:

> According to his terminology, Kirsanov would put it thus: "Every man is an egoist, including me. Now the question arises as to what is more in line with my interests, to go or to stay? If I go I suppress a private feeling. If I stay I risk outraging the feeling of my human dignity by the stupidity of a word or glance, motivated by this one feeling. This one feeling may be suppressed, and after some time my peace of mind will return. I will once again be content with my life. But if I act one time against all of my human nature, I will lose forever the possibility of peace of mind, the possibility of being content with myself. I will poison my whole life."[27]

According to "Kirsanov's theory of egoism," initiating an affair with Vera would be selfish, yet not quite selfish enough.[28] Retreat would leave his human dignity intact, which he decides is even more selfish, and thus preferable. Of course there is a more natural way of assessing this situation that is entirely disregarded: his sense of human dignity requires selfless action of him, and neither egoism nor reason has much to do with it at all. In any case Kirsanov decides that this time he will gradually fade out of the Lopukhovs's life. One would think this to be excruciating for Kirsanov, but no, "according to Kirsanov's theory, it is not excruciating but in fact even pleasant; after all, the more difficult a task, the more joy (as self-love) its successful completion brings you as you admire your own strength and skill."[29]

Vera Pavlovna's third dream

The good doctor's diagnosis proves correct: Vera is in love with Kirsanov and does not yet know it. It is her third dream that reveals the truth to her, when the dream goddess who has presided over the first two dreams compels Vera to read her diary out loud. Vera objects that she has never kept a diary, but a diary is produced all the same, and from it we learn that Vera respects Lopukhov and is grateful and loyal to him for saving her, but does not love him.[30] Waking, Vera sobs and begs Lopukhov to make love to her, apparently for the first time ever. After several years of chaste communal living, they finally consummate their marriage, and Vera tries to be a tender and attentive wife. But, using a term out of her second dream, the "chemistry" is wrong. At his insistence Vera tells Lopukhov about the dream that has so disturbed her (this time he has failed to divine it). Lopukhov the rationalist works out the love-triangle like a trigonometry problem in thirty minutes flat: Kirsanov loves Vera. Vera loves Kirsanov but has not yet guessed it. Kirsanov has guessed it and has been "selfishly" avoiding their company so as not to disturb their marriage. It is in Lopukhov's rationally selfish interest to sort out this mess, so he pays a visit to Kirsanov in the novel's best chapter: "A Theoretical Conversation."

When Lopukhov enters and declares that he must speak with Kirsanov, Kirsanov guesses that Lopukhov has guessed that Kirsanov has guessed what Vera has not yet guessed. Kirsanov tries to avoid this conversation, but Lopukhov explains, as one rational egoist to another, that he is only seeking his own selfish gain. What follows is a "theoretical" conversation concerning the happiness of a hypothetical person, perhaps a woman, where that person is either allowed to continue to live a satisfactory life, though possibly deficient in one aspect, or she is given the object of her desires, but at the risk of upsetting her peace of mind. Lopukhov wants Kirsanov to visit often and pursue his love for Vera. Kirsanov does not want to take the risk, so Lopukhov blackmails his friend into obeying his request by theorizing that if one hypothetical person guesses something about a second hypothetical person that the second would very much like to keep secret from a third, and if the first threatens to tell the third the second's secret, the first might force the second to do his bidding. At this, Kirsanov falls deep into thought, "staring at his fingers as if each one were an abstract hypothesis."[31] Kirsanov agrees to do what Lopukhov demands, causing the narrator to pop up like a referee and reassure the reader that both men are still technically within the rules of rational egoism, which has led them to a mutually advantageous situation: Kirsanov gets to be near the woman he loves and retains his dignity. Lopukhov finds a convenient exit from what has proven "a lost cause."[32] He can now stop wasting time courting Vera and flee while the fleeing is good. Indeed, if each of the two men examined his actions "as a theoretician," the narrator asserts, he would delight in observing "the sort of tricks that his egoism plays in practice."[33]

When Vera realizes that she loves Kirsanov, she confesses to Lopukhov, who tells her not to worry and promptly fakes his suicide. Now Rakhmetov enters the novel more fully, complete with a name. A special section, "A Different Sort of Person," tells Rakhmetov's biography in terms that evoke at once the hagiographical hero and the *bogatyr'* (the hero of the Russian folk epic or *bylina*).[34] He comes from an ancient clan whose twelfth-century Tatar progenitor was cut into pieces for trying to convert Russians to Islam. The reader gathers that Rakhmetov himself will probably die a martyr's death like his ancestor. Chernyshevsky shoots himself in the logical foot by creating his socialist "new person" in the image of Christ.

Rakhmetov was born into great wealth and owned thousands of serfs. At sixteen, beginning as a student at the University of Saint St. Petersburg, he was radicalized by Kirsanov, who told him which books to read. Rakhmetov's first epic feat is to read these tedious works—no doubt heaps of books by French and German socialist utopians and materialists. Three days in a row he reads, without breaking for sleep. The third night he drinks eight glasses of strong coffee. The fourth night no amount of coffee could help: "He fell to the floor and slept there for fifteen hours."[35] Waking, like the *bogatyr'* of yore from his preternaturally long sleep, he goes back to Kirsanov for more books. His friendship with Kirsanov and Lopukhov marks the beginning of his "rebirth."[36]

When he returns to his estate after two years of university courses, his family renounces him, presumably because of his new views. He wanders all over Russia in search of (socialist) adventure, meeting several young people whom he sends to Moscow University, providing them out of his own pocket with stipends so that they can study (and be revolutionaries). Maintaining great physical strength so that the peasants will respect him (plus, "it may come in handy"), Rakhmetov works various trades, hauls barges on the Volga, and eats as much as four men (mainly beefsteak).[37] During his first visit to the Lopukhov home, we see him polish off four pounds of black bread and an enormous chunk of ham, which he pulls out of his trousers pocket.

Though raised on fine food, Rakhmetov never allows himself wine or sweets. By contrast, Vera has a sweet tooth and drinks her tea with thick cream, which shows Rakhmetov to be made of sterner stuff. His rule, which would never have dawned on Vera, is that if the peasant does not eat it, he does not have the right either. The peasant eats black bread, apples but not apricots; Rakhmetov—ditto. He eats oranges in St. Petersburg, since the St. Petersburg peasantry eats oranges, but for a similar reason shuns oranges in the country. He has thought this out. There are, of course, those daily hunks of beef and ham, foods that are far too rich for the peasant's pocket, but he must make this exception in order to maintain his *bogatyr's* physique, ultimately for the peasant's own sake. His other indulgence is cigars, for which, like Lopukhov and Kirsanov, he has a sinful (bourgeois) passion. Rakhmetov suffers remorse for those damnable cigars, but he rationalizes them away with the excuse that he cannot think without smoking. Perhaps not, perhaps not. Unlike the Russian peasant, Rakhmetov has sworn off women too, and here hagiography seems the pertinent influence. Or perhaps Rakhmetov is exercising Malthusian celibacy to help slow population growth; Malthus is, by the way, one of the four writers Rakhmetov recognizes in the field of political economy.[38] When Rakhmetov pokes dozens of nails through a felt sheet and lies down on it for a night of agonizing sleep, lacerating his backside to the point where he must ask Kirsanov for "a sizeable quantity of ointment for the healing of wounds," we cannot blame Malthus: this desire to tame one's flesh comes directly from the lives of saints.[39] Even on normal nights, he sleeps on the floor with nothing but that felt sheet (sans nails) for comfort. What for?

Rakhmetov believes that he has no right to waste time. Therefore, he only reads "original" books. He rejects anything from the field of political economy beyond Malthus, John Stuart Mill, David Ricardo, and Adam Smith, because, he reasons, everybody else either distorts these four original writers or else repeats them. How he could know such a thing without further reading is a mystery he has no time to ponder. He reads William Thackeray's *Vanity Fair* and then joyfully chucks *Pendennis* after twenty pages, declaring that Thackeray had already said all he had in him with *Vanity Fair*. "Every book I read is selected," he chuckles, "so that it rids me of the need to read hundreds of other books."[40] So stingily does he economize time that he reads in order not to read.

What Rakhmetov lazily plunders from Adam Smith is the notion of the "invisible hand." When, in Book 4, Chapter 2 of *The Wealth of Nations*, Smith wrote famously of the "invisible hand," he elaborated a notion that Chernyshevsky would, less than a century later, distort into rational egoism.

> But the annual revenue of every society is always precisely equal to the exchangeable value of the whole annual produce of its industry, or rather is precisely the same thing with that exchangeable value. As every individual, therefore, endeavors as much as he can, both to employ his capital in the support of domestic industry, and so to direct that industry that its produce maybe of the greatest value; every individual necessarily labours to render the annual revenue of the society as great as he can. He generally, indeed, neither intends to promote the public interest, nor knows how much he is promoting it. By preferring the support of domestic to that of foreign industry, he intends only his own security; and by directing that industry in such a manner as its produce may be of the greatest value, he intends only his own gain; and he is in this, as in many other cases, led by an invisible hand to promote an end which was no part of his intention. Nor is it always the worse for the society that it was no part of it. By pursuing his own interest, he frequently promotes that of the society more effectually than when he really intends to promote it.[41]

Smith draws his conclusions from empirical data. The trader who seeks his own profit often unintentionally profits society as well.

How intrinsically different is the situation in Chernyshevsky's fantasy, where an awkwardly visible hand points the rational egoists toward utopia.

This then is the portrait of Rakhmetov, "a different sort of person," the "engine of engines," and "salt of the earth."[42] The final section of Chapter 3, entitled "Conversation with the Penetrating Reader and His Banishment," is one of the most awkward passages ever written. The narrator asks us to guess why the figure of Rakhmetov is necessary to the novel. Was it merely to convey Lopukhov's note to Vera after his fake suicide, revealing that he is still alive?[43] No, stupid reader, any episodic character could have served this mechanical function. The narrator eventually solves his own riddle: there are three levels of human existence. The reader occupies the lowest, a kind of "underworld slum." Vera, Kirsanov, and Lopukhov stand at ground level, and if the reader thought they were "hovering in the clouds," that is only because he himself is so far underground.[44] Rakhmetov exists at the lofty height where all people should and will be, once they adopt rational egoism and follow it like robots. Chernyshevsky once again invokes the metaphor of Plato's underground cave, in order to suggest that we too are prisoners in a cave mistaking the play of shadows for reality. As Lopukhov "freed" Vera, as Kirsanov "freed" Rakhmetov, so the narrator would "free" the reader. This authorial aside acts to pull readers into Vera's dream, whence rational egoism will release them into utopia.

By the end of the simulated suicide episode, Vera too has learned to play the rational egoism game. She claims in a letter to her "deceased husband" that if she did not deceive him with

Kirsanov, it was to advance her own selfish interest of not feeling "vile" about herself.[45] Guiltlessly rid of Lopukhov, remarried to her true love, Kirsanov, she enjoys the materialistic pleasures of frequent copulation, warm baths every morning, thick cream with tea twice a day, and corsetless dresses. After bringing into being a second sewing cooperative (eventually a third will materialize), she begins to study to become that model of a Russian nineteenth-century nihilist: a doctor. She must give up the thrills of socialistic commerce for medicine, which puts her professional life on a more securely materialistic and scientific footing. Only now she is ready for her final revolutionary dream.

Vera Pavlovna's fourth dream

Here, to an accompaniment of much narratorial smirking and winking, the happy socialists of the inevitable future perfect Vera's happy new life, indulging in an unceasing orgy of lazy feasting with frequent intermissions for promiscuous sex. The dream goddess of the first three dreams is back again in the role of mistress of ceremonies. In the midst of this "resplendent feast" of the future utopians, a poet stands up and reveals the secrets of human nature and history in eleven "pictures."[46] The women in the first three historical epochs, or "pictures," were oppressed and dissatisfied. By Picture 4, Chernyshevsky has, characteristically, forgotten the conceit of the poet and his pictures. Now the dream goddess addresses Vera directly, telling her that she came into existence when Jean Jacques Rousseau wrote *Julie or the New Heloise* (1761). Rousseau was the first to depict love in a novel as a romantic attraction of equals. In Picture 5, the goddess-*cum*-tour-guide finally dims the dazzling "halo" around her head and reveals her identity: she is Vera herself, but idealized and perfected, as seen through the eyes of her lover, Kirsanov. In this way Chernyshevsky adapts Feuerbach's idea of human godlikeness to his purposes. Picture 6 is not a picture at all but a kind of prose ode to the equality of the sexes. Picture 7 is missing, possibly removed by a merciful censor. Pictures 8 through 11 are more to the point. Here the dream goddess asks her sister, also a dream goddess, to take over the tour. She and Vera jump into the future and find themselves in London. It is the Crystal Palace from the World Fair of 1851, an edifice that Chernyshevsky had seen there during his travels of 1859. Only it has been rebuilt with improvements in a future socialist Russia. Vera sees a phalanstery with an outer shell of pig iron and crystal. Inside it is another building, constructed entirely of a shiny light new metal. Is it silver? Platinum? No, something much better: aluminum. "Ah," exclaims Vera, "I remember now, Sasha [Kirsanov] told me that sooner or later aluminum would replace wood, maybe stone, too" as a building material.[47] "But how sumptuous all this is!" she marvels, "Everywhere aluminum and more aluminum!"[48] The floors and ceilings, the furniture, the tableware are all aluminum.

As in the second dream, soil is an important theme here. It takes the shape of pretty fields of abundant grain and fruits surrounding the aluminum-and-crystal phalanstery. They must have installed good drainage. The same goes for another phalanstery, located in warmer Southern climes, where most of the utopians go for the winter. The dream goddess explains at great length how she inspired her worshippers to mix clay in with the sandy desert soil until, after many years, they had converted it to fertile, arable land. The attendant allegorical interpretation is that Russian people gradually evolved from bad soil to good, as they perfected their understanding of socialism and rational egoism. The socialist dream people have cleverly removed the need for a servant class and thus class conflict. How? The children work with the adults in the fields and do all the house chores! Never fear, though, for the dream goddess reassures Vera that "they really love it."[49]

But children are not what chiefly interests Chernyshevsky. The dream goddess is extremely anxious to show Vera how the adult socialists of the future amuse themselves after dinner. Some give vent to their creative side, singing, dancing, acting, reading, and engaging in other fulfilling activities. What about the others?

> Some are in the alleys of the garden, some are in their rooms, either to rest in solitude or with their children, but most of them, most of them—it's my secret. You saw in the great hall those burning cheeks and glimmering eyes. You saw—they kept leaving and coming. When they left—that was me, luring them away. Here the room of each man and each woman is my bower. There my secrets are inviolate. The curtains over the doors, the luxurious rugs that muffle all noise, a realm of silence and secrecy. When they returned, it was I returning them from the land of my secrets to these light amusements. Here I reign supreme.[50]

This "brothel within a phalanstery" is what so repulsed Herzen. The dream goddess's last words to Vera are "Strive to attain [this future]; work for it; bring it closer; transfer everything you can from it into the present."[51] Immediately following the fourth and final prophetic dream, we get an account, in minute detail, of one of Vera's sewing cooperatives: the building, the furniture, the furnishings, the seamstresses' bedrooms, their way of work and life, and their operating budget. The point of the parallel could not be any clearer. Vera has smuggled as much as she possibly could out of her utopian dream in order to set it in motion in her cooperative (and also in her private residence). This is the first earthly embodiment of the future socialist paradise.

Chernyshevsky's readers were likewise expected to "transfer" as much as they could from the novel to reality: feminism, free love, and rational egoism. But the most subversive of the novel's contrabands would prove to be the image of Rakhmetov, a mysterious blank that would, outside the bounds of the novel, get "filled in" with meanings Chernyshevsky could no longer control. Because Chernyshevsky was so logically inconsistent, he failed to realize that he had created in Rakhmetov, not a rational egoist, but a martyr designed to sacrifice himself for the collective. Taking their cue from Chernyshevsky, the Russian revolutionaries colored Rakhmetov a "mortus": a suicide terrorist. That story will continue in Chapter 4. Chapter 3 recounts Dostoevsky's violent encounter with *What Is to Be Done?*

3

Dostoevsky reborn

The Russian Idea

Dostoevsky returned from prison and exile to European Russia with a revelation that would become the foundation of his subsequent writing: the most basic necessity of mankind is freedom, the ultimate expression of freedom being self-sacrifice in the image of Christ. This put him at extreme odds with Chernyshevsky, who saw humans as determined by natural, social, and historical forces. True, in *What Is to Be Done?* Vera leaves the "basement" of social conditioning, escaping into the open air of socialism, but such expressions of freedom are understood to take place within the confines of a fixed historical process: the socialist future is inevitable, unquestioned. In 1861 Dostoevsky and his brother Mikhail got permission from the royal censor to begin publishing a journal they would call *Time* (*Vremia*). They wanted to position themselves between the Westernizers and Slavophiles, hoping to use *Time* as a means to make peace among the warring factions. The viewpoint the Dostoevskies attempted to convey in the new journal they called *Pochvenichestvo*, from the noun *pochva*, soil. The new platform might be translated into English as "The Soil Program" or even "Striving for the Soil." Naturally, they had in mind not some garden-variety dirt, and certainly not the socialist soil of Vera Pavlovna's dreams, but "The Russian Soil." This sometimes meant something as bland as the motherland, but, often assumed the cultic, pagan form of "the great wet mother earth." Here was a sloppy mystical concept that embraced Russian nationalism, ancient Slavic paganism, and an idiosyncratic revision of Christianity. You might say that what the Dostoevskies were proposing was a reactionary revolution.

This revolution was not anything like the one the radicals desired. Nor was it the bourgeois compromise, the "measured liberalism" that would so disgust Dostoevsky when he visited Western Europe in 1862. The Dostoevskies paradoxically wanted something more radical than the revolutionaries' wildest desire, and yet as reactionary as the Slavophiles' most retrograde fantasy: a revolution that would take the Russian people back into an idealized, spiritualized, mythologized past, laden with the finest gifts of the enlightened present. They proposed to mend a rift between the educated but godless aristocracy and the religious but ignorant peasantry; the rebirth of the entire Russian people under Christ; the religious grounding of the elite in the Russian soil; the transfiguration of the peasantry in the light of education. It goes without saying this program's chances for success were not stellar.

"We are living in an era that is remarkable and critical in the highest degree," Dostoevsky declared in his first call to subscribe to *Time*.[1] The year was 1860, the eve of the emancipation. A great "revolution" was afoot:

> This revolution is the convergence of the educated class . . . with the people and the initiation of the entire great Russian people into all elements of our current life; the Russian people, who turned away from Peter's reforms 170 years ago and who up to this day have lived their own unique and independent life apart from the educated class. . . . The reforms of Peter the Great . . . have cost us too dearly. They separated us from the people. From the very start the people rejected them. The ways of life foisted upon the people by means of this transformation answered neither to their spirit nor to their aspirations. . . . The people called the new ways German and the followers of the great czar—foreigners.[2]

And so the Russian people trudged along in the dark for centuries, trying to find their own way forward, stumbling into "secret ugly sects," yet always preserving what Dostoevsky called their spiritual "energy" (something the educated class had squandered ages ago). Utterly lost in Western ways of life, the *intelligentsia* had finally grasped the fact that it could not "squeeze itself into some Western form of life."

> We have become convinced finally that we too are a distinct nationality, indigenous in the highest degree, and that our task is to create for ourselves a new form, our own form, a native

form, one taken from our own soil, taken from the people's spirit and principles. No, not conquered do we return to our native soil. We do not renounce our past: we understand its reasons.[3]

Dostoevsky explains that the educated class had been forced to depart from its native soil for a time, to step outside of itself, as it were, in order to look back upon its homeland with some measure of objectivity. Now it is returning to the soil and to the Russian people, but returning with an enlightened awareness of the place of privilege Russia must occupy in the "great family of all nations."

And now he trots out the "Russian Idea," which "will perhaps be the synthesis of all those ideas which Europe is developing in its separate nationalities." The great hope that defines the Russian Idea is that "perhaps all that is inimical in these ideas will find a peaceful existence in the further development of the Russian people."[4] Educated Russians have tried and failed to become Western Europeans, but the process has transformed them into superhumans, endowed with the hard-won ability to speak all languages, to understand all the disparate national ideas, to unite all of this in themselves, and to add to this recipe a secret ingredient of their own: the spiritual life of the Russian peasants. Now the goal is for the educated class and the peasantry to come together in mutual understanding. For the accomplishment of this task, educated Russia must get busy "exploiting its position and exploiting it intensively" in order to educate the peasantry. Otherwise, Dostoevsky adds, the peasantry will never understand them! "The spread of intensive education, as quickly as possible and at any cost."[5] Such is the program. Dostoevsky's repeated use of the word "intensive" is telling. After forcing them to accept the Petrine reforms, forcing them to accept a new form of religion, forcing them to live as slaves, the privileged class is now to force the peasants to fall in line with the Soil Program. The Russian Idea depended on their cooperation.

Dostoevsky seems to have had in mind something similar to the vision of *sobornost* that his contemporary, the Slavophile philosopher Aleksey Komyakov, described as Russia's ancient past and future salvation: *sobornost* was Komyakov's word for a religious "togetherness" or, literally, "collective," of the Russian people, a commune based upon the historical *obshchina* or *mir*. This was an Orthodox village collective that had the power to decide disputes and distribute land among the peasants. To Komyakov's vision of a peasant collective under czar and God, Dostoevsky applies his own stroke: the European Enlightenment, which he would under no circumstances relinquish. Dostoevsky does not confront the fact that it was the Enlightenment that led to another conception of collectivism under the banner of utilitarianism, materialism, and socialism. We may as well refer to this opposing form of collectivism as the Western Idea.

As for the goal of mediating between the radicals and reactionaries, *Time* was an abject failure. In part this was due to the inherent contradictions of the Russian Idea, which, on the one hand, tried, impossibly, to edit the Western Idea out of the Enlightenment, and, on the other hand, tried, again impossibly, to broaden the traditional peasant collective enough so that it could embrace the great achievements of Western literature, art, and philosophy. The other reason for the failure of *Time* was that the Dostoevskies were all too willing to take potshots at the radicals' two sacred cows, Chernyshevsky and Dobrolyubov. Against Dobrolyubov, Dostoevsky argued, "A work without artistic value can never and in no way attain its goal; moreover, it does more harm than good to its cause; hence the Utilitarians in neglecting artistic value, are the first to harm their own cause."[6] This was essentially the same argument made by the censor who allowed Chernyshevsky's novel to be published. Like the censor, Dostoevsky was wrong—it did not hurt the cause. The radical critics demanded that artists ignore formal considerations in the attempt to bring good and just content to the world, and Dostoevsky pointed out the irony of freedom-loving critics denying authors the very artistic freedom that they purported to defend. No, replied Dostoevsky,

> art is for man just as much a necessity as eating or drinking. The need for beauty and the creations embodying it are inseparable from man, and without it man would perhaps have no wish to live. Man thirsts for [beauty] . . . and herein, perhaps, lies the greatest mystery of artistic creation, that the image of beauty which emerges from its hands immediately becomes an idol.[7]

This notion—that people read in order to idolize the image they discover in books—is essential in accounting for the destructive power of bad literature.

The fires

During the spring of 1862 fires broke out in St. Petersburg. The proclamation "Young Russia" had just appeared, calling for the ruthless dismantling of the political and social structures of Russia. When the Bazaar (*Tolkuchii rynok*) burned in the spring of 1862, many thought that the fires were a direct response to this call to rebellion. It has proved impossible to establish whether or not that was the case, but it is now known that the author of the proclamation was Pyotr Zaichnevsky. He had written it in prison in 1861, much as Chernyshevsky would write *What Is to Be Done?* about a year later in prison. Though Zaichnevsky and Chernyshevsky were apparently not acquainted, Chernyshevsky had profoundly influenced Zaichnevsky with his populist ideas. Zaichnevsky belonged to the tradition of Russian Jacobinists and Blanquists and advocated the use of terrorism and secret societies to overthrow the czarist regime.[8] Whether or not Chernyshevsky himself was a Jacobinist is a matter for conjecture. Dostoevsky reasoned that Chernyshevsky must be at the center of a secret terrorist organization, for as the fires raged on he decided he had to confront Chernyshevsky. There are three remarkable accounts of their meeting. The first was written by Dostoevsky and appears in an entry of his *Diary of Writer* from 1873. Dostoevsky recalls, eleven years after the fact, that he awoke one morning to find "Young Russia" hanging from the lock of his door. The proclamation outraged him with its incendiary content and with its crudely stupid form. That evening Dostoevsky decided to call on Chernyshevsky at his apartment. Chernyshevsky answered the door, and Dostoevsky handed him the proclamation, asking,

"Nikolai Gavrilovich, what is this?"

"Yes, but what is your point?"

"Can they really be this stupid and laughable? Can't they be made to stop and to desist in this filth?"

"Do you really suspect that I am in league with them, that I could have participated in the composition of this pamphlet?"[9]

Dostoevsky assured Chernyshevsky that he had no such suspicions but suggested that Chernyshevsky's influence with the authors of the proclamation might be sufficient to make them stop. Chernyshevsky replied that he did not even know any of the authors and that his hypothetical intercession might not produce a result, adding that such phenomena as the proclamations were "inevitable." At this point another visitor arrived, interrupting their conversation, and Dostoevsky left. A few days later Chernyshevsky returned Dostoevsky's visit, calling on him at his apartment. He stayed an hour, was very gentile and courteous, and Dostoevsky had the impression he wanted to strike up an acquaintance. This, however, was not to be. Soon after Dostoevsky went on a trip to Moscow, and during his absence Chernyshevsky was arrested and exiled. Dostoevsky never saw Chernyshevsky again; he had already died before Chernyshevsky was allowed to return from Siberia.

It is amusing to observe how different Chernyshevsky's version of their meeting is, in matters of both fact and impression.

Chernyshevsky gave his coldly detached, pseudo-medical account in 1888, seven years after Dostoevsky's death and twenty-six years after the event in question. According to him, Dostoevsky suddenly materialized in his sitting room looking very troubled and flustered and without so much as a how-do-you-do blurted out his conviction that Chernyshevsky was on close terms with the arsonists, and urgently requested that he use his influence with them to make them desist.

> I had heard that Dostoevsky's nerves were deranged to a point of unruliness that approached mental disorder, but I had not imagined that his sickness had reached such a state that he could associate me with the arson at the Bazaar. Seeing that the mental disarray of the poor patient was of the sort that causes medics to warn against contradicting the unfortunate sufferer and to prescribe saying anything necessary to calm him, I replied, "Very well, Fyodor Mikhailovich, I shall do as you wish."[10]

According to Chernyshevsky, he had never met Dostoevsky until this very moment and only recognized him from portraits. This was not true. They had met before, as Dostoevsky more accurately pointed out in his recollection. Chernyshevsky claims that he fulfilled the minimum requirements of common courtesy, asking about *Time*, but that Dostoevsky, failing to take the hint, stayed for two hours, prattling on and on about his journal. Put out by his unwanted guest, Chernyshevsky says he did not even bother to listen to Dostoevsky's reply.

For Dostoevsky, the visit was a pleasant meeting of two leading literary lights, while for Chernyshevsky it was the sad case of a mentally deranged "patient" importuning his healthy interlocutor with self-indulgent ramblings. Since Chernyshevsky's account was written much later than Dostoevsky's and contains a verifiable error, one is inclined to take Dostoevsky as being closer to the truth. Chernyshevsky may have misremembered for a reason: envy. Dostoevsky was not only a far better writer than Chernyshevsky, he had even beaten Chernyshevsky to revolutionary activity by nearly fifteen years.

The third account actually belongs to a fictional character, Fyodor Godunov-Cherdyntsev, the protagonist of Nabokov's novel, *The Gift* (1937). Here is Nabokov's amusing version of the fateful meeting:

> Whit Monday (May 28, 1862), a strong wind is blowing; a conflagration has begun on the Ligovka and then the desperadoes set fire to the Apraxin Market. Dostoevski is running, firemen are galloping. . . . And over there, thick smoke billows over the Fontanka canal in the direction of Chernyshyov Street, where presently a new, black column arises. . . . Meanwhile Dostoevski has arrived. He has arrived at the heart of the *blackness*, at Chernyshevski's place, and starts to beg him hysterically to *put a stop* to all this. Two aspects are interesting here: the belief in Nikolay Gavrilovich's satanic powers, and the rumors that the arson was being carried out according to the same plan which the Petrashevskians had drawn up as early as 1849.
>
> Secret agents, in tones also not void of mystic horror, reported that during the night at the height of the disaster "laughter was heard coming from Chernyshevski's window."[11]

While Nabokov makes an utter mockery of Chernyshevsky's life and works, he does not spare Dostoevsky either but instead reminds us that Dostoevsky was himself a reformed revolutionary. More importantly, as I show in Chapter 7, Nabokov faults both of them for being ideologues instead of artists.

"The Crocodile"

The fires raged not only in the streets of St. Petersburg, but on the pages of the journals. The Westernizers were slugging it out with the Slavophiles, and the Dostoevsky brothers were caught in the middle. The czar's censor shut down their journal *Time* in 1863 because of a controversial article written by Nikolai Strakhov, but in 1864 the brothers were permitted to start up a new journal. They called it *Epoch* (*Epokha*) so that its connection with *Time* would be clear, but Mikhail Dostoevsky died later that year, leaving Fyodor heavily in debt, the sole party responsible for the bookkeeping, editing, editorializing, composition of short stories, and amusements and book reviews. The debt and workload were soon to prove too much for him, but Dostoevsky managed to publish two remarkable new works of literature in *Epoch* before it too was shut down: his first real masterpiece, *Notes from the Underground* (1864), and the unfinished entertainment, "Crocodile" (1865). The latter appeared in the very last issue of *Epoch*, which the authorities closed immediately thereafter. As one can tell by its full title, "The Crocodile, An Unusual Event, or an Incident in the Arcade, the True Story of a Gentleman of a Certain Age and a Certain Appearance Who Was Swallowed

Alive and Whole without Any Scraps by an Arcadian Crocodile and of What Came of This" is a light-hearted satire or, as Dostoevsky called it, a "naughty literary prank."[12]

In it a government official named Ivan Matveich takes his wife to see a crocodile in the Arcade (*Пассаж*), a fashionable shopping mall on Nevsky Prospect. A German and his mother are showing the beast there for a fee, and when Ivan Matveich gets too close to the crocodile, it suddenly swallows him whole. Unwilling merely to die and be digested, Ivan Matveich begins to speak from the crocodile's belly, and not simply to speak, but to espouse the latest radical ideas. When his wife suggests cutting open the crocodile's belly, Ivan Matveich forbids it, pointing out that the reptile is the German's property and that Russians must proceed first of all from "economic principles" if they are to attract foreign capital and join the world economy.[13] Many of Dostoevsky's contemporaries, in particular his ideological opponents, straight away saw in this "prank" an evil allegory aimed at Chernyshevsky, who had been "swallowed up" in 1862 by the Peter and Paul Fortress, whence he began to give voice to the most radical ideas, writing *What Is to Be Done?*[14] But Ivan Matveich is not at all the "unhappy prisoner" that the narrator takes him to be, and when the narrator, proposes that now is the time for weeping, not courage, Ivan Matveich replies,

> No! . . . For I am absolutely boiling over with great ideas. Only now do I have the leisure to dream about the improvement of the destiny of all mankind. Truth and light will now issue forth from this crocodile. I shall certainly invent my own

new theory of new economic relations and I will take pride in it—which I never before had the time to do because of my government job and trashy society amusements. I shall overturn everything and become a new Fourier.[15]

Formerly, nobody had ever listened to him, but now that he is a prisoner (inside a crocodile) his "every word will be heard, every utterance pondered, broadcast, published."[16] Ivan Matveich also has plans for his flirtatious wife, who is to run a cultural salon, thus increasing her husband's new fame. The new Fourier's wife struck contemporaries as an obvious and cruel satire of Chernyshevsky's attractive, frivolous, and extremely unfaithful wife, Olga.

Dostoevsky let the rumors about "The Crocodile" fly for many years before he finally tried to lay them to rest. In the issue of *Diary of a Writer* for 1873, Dostoevsky published a denial that his "Crocodile" was a satire of Chernyshevsky and expressed regret that he had waited so long to come out with the truth about the episode. It is here that Dostoevsky describes his meetings with Chernyshevsky, including the incident during the fire in 1862 and insists that their relations had always been cordial. He also states emphatically that as one who had suffered the very same indignities and torments that Chernyshevsky was enduring—imprisonment in the Peter and Paul Fortress, mock execution, exile to Siberia, and forced labor—he would have been incapable of insulting Chernyshevsky in the impugned manner. It is hard to discern the truth in this matter, but the rumor did damage to Dostoevsky's reputation among progressives and actually caused an outraged ideological opponent to write a negative review of *Crime and Punishment*, which he later admitted to admiring.[17]

Notes from the Underground

But already *Notes from the Underground*, which had appeared a year before "The Crocodile," had sealed Dostoevsky's reputation as a retrograde and enemy as far as the radicals were concerned. It was also a milestone that marked a new period in Dostoevsky's life: his parents were dead. Pushkin was dead. Gogol was dead. Siberia was behind him. His first wife Maria would die in April of 1864, as he was writing the second half of *Notes from the Underground*. His brother Mikhail would die the month after its publication. It would be an exaggeration to say that the old Dostoevsky was dead: the narrator, or "underground man," is related to the dreamer-narrator of "White Nights" (1848) and to Golyadkin in "The Double" (1846). He has some of the color of a whole line of "superfluous men" who begin with Alexander Griboedov's Chatsky, Pushkin's Eugene Onegin, and Mikhail Lermontov's Pechorin. But *Notes from the Underground* is sooner a radical departure than a further development. Dostoevsky's works from the 1840s had presented a struggle caused by an unjust society that crushed "poor folk." The new works would retain some sympathy for the "insulted and injured," but now the struggle was not an external one between the individual and society but rather internal, as man tries to find an answer to the egoism raging within his own breast.[18] Most immediately Dostoevsky's underground narrator is a direct answer to

Chernyshevsky's "new people": to Rakhmetov, the revolutionary "man of action," and to Lopukhov and Kirsanov, both of whom "save" women by marrying them to socialism and to themselves.

What Is to Be Done? played a decisive role in making Dostoevsky a great novelist. It provoked *Notes from the Underground* and the four great novels that capitalized on the discoveries of his new "underground" style. The polemic with *What Is to Be Done?* is quite clear, starting with the plot itself. *Notes from the Underground* is the story of a man, the narrator, who refuses to rescue a former prostitute whom he has persuaded to leave the brothel. *What Is to Be Done?* had developed this very theme in the person of the former prostitute, Nastasya Kriukova, whom Kirsanov converts to socialism. She later turns up in Vera's sewing cooperative, acting as a stand-in for Vera herself, saved by Lopukhov from an arranged marriage to a scoundrel (a version of prostitution deemed acceptable among the bourgeoisie). The rescued prostitute had in fact become something of a literary *cliché* by the time Dostoevsky wrote his novella. This is evident from the narrator's choice of Nekrasov's poem "When from the Gloom of Error" (1846) as epigraph for Part II of the novella:

When from the gloom of error,
With heated words of persuasion,
I rescued your fallen soul,
And all full of deep torment,
Wringing your hands, you cursed
The vice that had ensnared you,
When, torturing with reminiscence

Your forgetful conscience,
You told me the story
Of everything that had preceded me,
And suddenly, covering your face with your hands,
Full of shame and horror,
You dissolved in a torrent of tears,
Indignant, stunned . . .
Etc., etc. etc.[19]

The narrator once believed in all this romantic tripe but now obviously holds it in contempt. I say romantic even though Chernyshevsky and Nekrasov are supposed to be "realists," and, as it were, grown-ups. The continuation of Nekrasov's poem, which the derisive etceteras cut off, is as follows:

Believe me: I harkened not without sympathy,
I thirstily caught each sound . . .
I understood it all, o child of misfortune!
I forgave it all and forgot it all.

. . .

Grieving for nothing, fruitlessly,
Warm not a serpent in your breast
And enter my house boldly and freely
As the rightful lady of the house!

The methodological breakthrough for Dostoevsky resulted from his argument with Chernyshevsky and other socialists, and this polemical edge is visible in so many aspects of Dostoevsky's novella. Mikhail Bakhtin called the innovation "dialogism," meaning that the underground narrator never makes a statement without some ideological opponent in mind. He is always arguing in anticipation of another's word, another's thought, another's belief system; moreover, he has, at various times in his life, cherished all of these ideas himself, and while he eventually rejected them, they have taken up permanent residence in his brain as internal antagonists. This explains the narrator's pugnacious, sarcastic, and yet self-belittling tone. But the new style is more than mere tone: from now on, Dostoevsky's characters will be fashioned in accordance with their ideas. Starting with *Notes from the Underground*, Dostoevsky's heroes and "antiheroes," as he calls his underground narrator, are but personifications of various ideologies. Chernyshevsky was not Dostoevsky's only opponent; the target is the Western Idea in its entirety. But Chernyshevsky had to bear the brunt of Dostoevsky's anger because he was the one who brought this trend into sharp relief in the Russian intellectual life of the early 1860s. It is not merely that Chernyshevsky was close at hand; it is also that he was so wildly popular, as Dostoevsky observed with growing alarm.

While the message of *What Is to Be Done?* was painfully obvious, Dostoevsky takes pains to hide his meanings in *Notes from the Underground*. One thing that is not at all concealed, however, is his disgust at the *naiveté* of rational egoism, which he neatly defines as the "theory of the renewal of the human species by means of a system of personal gain."[20]

O, tell me, who was it who first announced, who first proclaimed, that man does nasty things only because he does not know his true interests, and that if he were enlightened, if his eyes were opened to his true, normal interests, then man would immediately stop doing nasty things, would immediately become good and noble, because being enlightened and understanding where his true interest lies, he would see that his own interest lies in goodness, and it's well known that there is not one man who can act knowingly against his own personal gain, ergo, so to speak, he would be compelled to do good deeds? O, the babe! O, the pure, innocent child![21]

The narrator's rebuttal of this simplistic idea is quite effective:

For goodness' sake, when, in the first place, throughout all these past millennia, has man acted only out of his own interest? What do we do with the millions of instances that bear witness to the fact that people knowingly, that is, fully comprehending their true interest, left it in the background and rushed in a different direction, choosing risk, gambling without being forced by anyone, as if precisely because they did not wish to take the indicated route, and stubbornly, willfully blazed another trail—a difficult one, an absurd one, almost seeking it out in the dark. Look, that means stubbornness and willfulness pleased them more than any sort of gain. . . . Gain! What is gain anyway? And can you really take it upon yourself to define precisely what is in a man's best interest? And what if it turns out one's best interest *at certain moments* not only can but indeed must lie precisely in a certain case in wishing oneself harm and not gain? But if this is so, if this case can exist, then the whole principle goes up in smoke.

What do you think? Does such a case exist? You are laughing, gentlemen. Well, go ahead and laugh, but answer me: are your gains calculated with absolute precision? Does there not exist some kind of advantage that failed to fit and indeed cannot fit into any system of classification?[22]

This mysterious advantage, more advantageous than all the others advantages, turns out to be free will. At any rate free will is the exalted term for it; the exasperating narrator always exercises freedom in a debased form, as whimsy or stupidity or better yet (his favorite word) "spite." By spite he means something both whimsical and stupid—with a dash of wickedness thrown in for spice.

Dostoevsky had read Marquis de Sade, who paints a much more realistic picture than Chernyshevsky of the consequences of constructing morality upon the foundation of egoism. Sade's novel *Justine, or the Misfortunes of Virtue* (1791), written, like *What Is to Be Done?*, in prison, depicts man as happy only when his schemes and calculations allow him to triumph over others. Sade, in his novel, savors again and again the pleasures of the egoist: rape, theft, and murder; and as the maniacs who abuse Justine explain to her, their joy in evil is intensified and perfected by their consciousness of the suffering it causes her. While the pursuit of monstrous pleasures is not necessarily an exclusively rational enterprise, *Justine* moves according to an iron logic which is perpetually made to demonstrate that selfish vice will always win out over selfless virtue. What is more, Sade's criminals are consummate in their application of reason— usually in the form of cunning and calculation—to attain their end. Dostoevsky knew this well, and so does his underground "anti-hero," who points out that history is replete with examples of the disastrous consequences of people pursuing selfish gain. Reason, he adds, has hardly ever been the motor of humanity. Dostoevsky and Sade share the instinct that a society will descend into a maelstrom of viciousness and cruelty should each individual pursue selfish gain. Adam Smith's invisible hand might play a role in the smooth functioning of imports and exports, but if this hand is allowed to dominate all levels of human interaction it will become a fist and smash everything to smithereens. This is a vision of anarchy that delighted Sade and horrified Dostoevsky, but at least they both had realistic instincts for the mechanics of selfishness.

While Dostoevsky's underground man does not glory in destruction the way Sade's miscreants do, he would almost certainly prefer universal destruction to the society Chernyshevsky smirkingly reveals in his aluminum utopia, which is really a type of prison. What Dostoevsky abominated most in rational egoism was the implication that man is but the plaything of "scientifically" ascertainable laws: the laws of nature, the laws of historical "progress," the laws of sociology, the laws of psychology. When confronted by the rational egoist slave, the narrator's instinct is to spit in the face of reason and act on whim. On a deeper level the novella shows that living by caprice and spite, always acting against one's interest, is yet another trap, the prison of the underground.

Still, the narrator's parody of Chernyshevsky's novel is masterful. *Notes from the Underground* begins with the narrator's famous declaration that he is sick and that, while he respects medicine, he refuses to go to a doctor out of spite. He acknowledges that in behaving in such an absurd fashion he will only harm himself, but so be it. Rational egoism insists that people will always seek out their selfish interest, whether in the avoidance of suffering or in the acquisition of material advantage.

> When they prove to you that one drop of your own fat must be more precious to you than a hundred thousand fellow creatures and that this result resolves all of your so-called virtues and duties and prejudices and other rubbish, just go ahead and accept it; there's nothing you can do about it, because two times two is mathematics. Just you try to object.[23]

Naturally, the narrator does object. He resents the fact that these sociologists, positivists, and "scientists" are studying the mind and seeking out its norms so that all thoughts and actions might be calculated like the figures of an algorithmic table or the stops on a train schedule. His revolt is an attempt to jump off the algorithmic table. Apart from selfishness, the narrator feels a great multitude of contradictory elements roiling within and demanding expression—a need that he has suppressed all his life up until the moment when he takes plume in hand to write his "Notes." Words like "contradiction," "paradox," and "negation" abound in this novella as a result of the narrator's belligerent attitude toward rational egoism, but the word that best characterizes his worldview, his most advantageous advantage, is spite.

Out of spite he wages war for years with a certain petitioner to the department of the civil service where he works, an officer who rattles his saber in a particularly annoying way. Out of spite he dreams for too many years of avenging himself upon another officer who will not make way for him on the sidewalk whenever they meet. Finally, in order to establish his equality, he compels himself to bump shoulders with this absurd nemesis of his. This shoulder-bumping episode, by the way, is a direct parody of a passage in *What Is to Be Done?*, where Lopukhov makes a rule for himself that he will never yield to another man on the sidewalk. When some big shot bumps into him and calls him a "swine," Lopukhov, displaying icy sangfroid and Übermensch strength, picks his antagonist up and carefully places him in a canal.[24] Note that Chernyshevsky's heroes do not experience complicated emotions like spite. When the underground man humiliates himself at a farewell dinner for a school comrade named Zverkov, it is spite that makes him do it. Later that evening, again out of spite he delivers a "pathetic speech" to a prostitute, Liza, cajoling her to leave the bordello and come to his apartment so that he can "rescue" her, like one of Chernyshevsky's heroes. But he is no Lopukhov, and, finally, when she does in fact come, he insults her and chases her away.

His cruel treatment of Liza at the end of the story returns the reader to the beginning, to his first words, "I am a sick man." You might call this sickness "spite," but it is a kind of spite that always hurts the subject, a spite of perversity. It is the impulse to do what is certain to harm you the most despite—and even because of—your knowledge of what is in your best interest. The root of this sickness is consciousness. "The more I was aware of goodness and about all that is 'noble and lofty,'" he says, "the deeper I sank into my swamp."[25] Chernyshevsky's view of the human mind is far too simplistic. In the first place, consciousness is much more than reason alone. In the second, it is more complicated: a person's very awareness of his best interest may perversely persuade him to do the opposite. Spite and perverseness are approximate descriptions of the narrator's sickness. "Irrational egoism" would be more precise.

One of Dostoevsky's most elegant inventions in *Notes from the Underground* is an architectural trope that organizes the novella's symbols and imagery. The narrator understands the laws of nature to be a wall before which unreflective men— contemptuously dismissed by the narrator as "men of action"— stop, fully satisfied that they can go no farther. A more intelligent man, understanding that he cannot ram his head through this wall, resents it with all his might for the rest of his absurd life. Chernyshevsky's utopia is constructed of just such walls, since it is the laws of nature, society, psychology, and history that will inexorably lead to the Palace of Crystal and Aluminum, to child labor, to amateur choirs, and to unfettered fornication. Through the underground narrator's satire, however, this false utopia is deconstructed.

> You believe in a crystal edifice that is eternally unshakable, that is in an edifice at which you could never stick out your tongue on the sly. . . . Well, perhaps I am afraid of this edifice for the very reason that it is crystal and eternally unshakable

and that you won't even be able to stick your tongue out at it on the sly.

Don't you see: if it's a chicken coop instead of a palace and it starts to rain, I will perhaps crawl into the chicken coop in order not to get drenched, but I will still not mistake the chicken coop for a palace out of gratitude for saving me from the rain. You laugh, you even say, "in that case chicken coops and palatial residences are the same thing." "Yes," I reply, "if our sole end in living was not to get wet."[26]

To paraphrase, if the socialists succeed in building their utopia as the ideal home for a life that satisfies exclusively material needs, they will have created nothing more than a coop for human chickens.

The implication: trying to live in order to meet material needs alone is not only a vulgar endeavor but a stupid one and ultimately doomed since people also have other needs. The underground man would be too embarrassed to use words like "spiritual" or "religious," but he comes very close to it, saying that he yearns for an edifice at which one could never stick out one's tongue on the sly. In architectural terms, that edifice might look something like the Russian Orthodox Church. In a more basic sense, the narrator has forgotten about brotherly love. Dostoevsky the Ideologue would say that as a member of the intelligentsia, the underground narrator has become detached from the Russian soil and suffers as a result of his estrangement from the people and their traditions. The "underground"—literally "underfloor"—is a visualization of the rejection of the

Crystal Palace. Instead of joining Vera and the other socialists romping on the main level of their phalanstery, the underground man prefers to sit out all that embarrassing awkwardness in the basement. While readers can admire his dignity in opting out, they can also see that living in a hole in the ground is a bad mistake.

Chernyshevsky's system is profoundly deterministic, but consistently acting against your interests is not less so. The underground man allows himself to be defined by the worldview he rejects. Unlike Chernyshevsky, Dostoevsky believed in free will. In the Christian vein, he thought that all good things spring from freedom, but not the debased freedom of caprice or spite: what Dostoevsky had in mind was the paradoxical Christian freedom that comes of sacrificing selfish desires. That self-sacrifice is the highest form of freedom is a revelation which eludes the underground narrator and, one gathers, the very truth for which he yearns.

Self-sacrifice is the official bugaboo of rational egoism, and it will later be again under objectivism, but we have seen that Rakhmetov and his austere "rigorism" strongly evoke martyrdom all the same. The revolutionary terrorists of the 1860s could see this, too, and so the historical manifestation of Rakhmetovism in the immediate aftermath of the publication of *What Is to Be Done?* became the terrorist-suicide, or "mortus"—not at all the sort of self-sacrifice Dostoevsky had in mind.

4

Rigor "Mortus" or waiting for Rakhmetov

Dostoevsky had foreseen that Chernyshevsky's book would exert a disastrous influence on Russia, and events did begin to thicken in its immediate aftermath. Nikolai Ishutin formed a revolutionary circle in 1863, the very year *What Is to Be Done?* was published in *The Contemporary*. Georgy Plekhanov's remark that "in each of the prominent Russian revolutionaries there was a huge share of Rakhmetovism" was an apt characterization of Ishutin, who painstakingly attempted to re-create himself in the image of Rakhmetov.[1] It was said of Ishutin that he acknowledged three great men in all human history: Jesus, St. Paul, and Chernyshevsky.[2] His followers, too, lived lives of voluntary privation, sleeping on the floor and devoting themselves to revolutionary activity. Within two years of the publication of *What Is to Be Done?*, inspired by Vera Pavlovna's sewing cooperative, they established a commune in Moscow that included a mutual-aid society, a sewing cooperative and book-binding cooperative, a free library, and a free school. Vera Zasulich worked for a time in the Ishutin book bindery, and her sisters and mother joined the sewing cooperative. (Despite the commercial successes of the fictional cooperatives, their real-life correlatives quickly failed through the incompetence and inattentiveness of their members.)

Ishutin's circle, known as "The Organization," deployed the Jesuit principle of rings within rings that we have already associated with Nikolai Speshnev. A socialist named Ivan Khudiakov had traveled to Geneva and returned in 1866 to tell Ishutin about a European Revolutionary Committee, which Khudiakov may or may not have invented. Khudiakov insisted that the Committee was prepared to arm revolutionary groups across Europe with bombs for the purpose of regicide.[3] According to the files of the secret police, Khudiakov did occupy a key position in a terror network that stretched from Western Europe to the Far East. He maintained contact with Herzen, Polish separatists, and *The Contemporary*. Khudiakov had made concrete arrangements to liberate Chernyshevsky from his Siberian exile in order that he (Chernyshevsky) might lead the revolution.[4] At this point, according to a version of events I find compelling, an inner circle of The Organization formed. The name of this inner ring was "Hell," and its members were ascetic terrorists living under strict revolutionary discipline. In the pursuit of their goals, everything was permitted: deception, denunciation, theft, infiltration, extortion, blackmail, and murder.[5] The members took an oath requiring them to kill anybody who refused to follow orders.[6] They accepted that the means of emancipation was terror, specifically the assassination of the czar and of his officials. Serial assassination was one of their approved methods: if the heir did not take the assassination of his parent to heart and agree to reform, then he would be next on the hit list.

Another idea that arose in the Ishutinite system of terror was that the regicide might later become a suicide. In the inner circles of Hell, secrets were profound, and misunderstandings could arise. During a late-night conversation involving Ishutin and three of his followers, P. F. Nikolaev, P. D. Ermalov, and V. N. Shaganov, one of them invented a word, *mortus*. It seems that the initiates themselves were confused about whether the word *mortus* was a joke or to be taken with deadly seriousness.[7] "I can't remember who used the word first," Nikolaev later claimed at his trial, "It was said while we were joking around, and it could not have entered my mind that such a conversation would be taken for a serious plot. . . . Maybe it's a subject about which you can't even joke."[8] It goes without saying that one must regard with at least some skepticism the words of the Ishutinites spoken in court or during interrogation at the hands of the secret police. On trial the plotters were obviously doing their best to conceal deeper meanings and lead the prosecution astray. In hindsight it is clear that *mortus* was meant to signify not merely a czaricide, but a czaricide-suicide, a concept that was certainly discussed in Hell.[9] Rakhmetov was probably the inspiration, as he was for so much of the Ishutinites' way of thought and life. In Hell, Rakhmetov's "rigorism" is understood to be austere ideological and physical discipline, the use of conspiratorial methods, and devotion to the cause of revolution even to the point of murder or suicide.

Ishutin's cousin Dmitry Karakozov nominated himself to become Hell's first *mortus*. Karakozov had been expelled from Moscow University in early 1866 and was dejected and even suicidal. He was also quite ill and told his co-conspirators that killing the czar and then himself was his only way out.[10] In February of 1866, Karakozov traveled to St. Petersburg and met with Khudiakov, who may have supplied him with a pistol. On April 4, 1866, at the gates of the Summer Garden, Karakozov made an attempt on Czar Alexander II. As he was pulling the trigger, a peasant struck his arm, saving the czar's life. Karakozov fell immediately into the hands of the czar's guards, who found in his gun a second cartridge, which, for some reason, he had not even attempted to fire. On his person they also found a syringe with strychnine and morphine and a bottle of prussic acid. Apparently the plan was to kill the czar and then attempt to flee. Upon a successful escape, Karakozov would disfigure his face and assume a false identity. If capture and arrest appeared inevitable, then it was to be suicide by lethal injection. Nothing went off right for Karakozov: after his arrest he asked for forgiveness and converted to Russian Orthodoxy. Five months later he was hanged.

Nechaev would call this assassination attempt "the beginning of our sacred cause."[11] There is a beginning, however, that precedes the one identified by Nechaev, and that is Chernyshevsky's novel.

The Supreme Criminal Court plausibly concluded that Karakozov had acted according to Hell's *mortus* scheme under the influence of *What Is to Be Done?*[12] The Karakozovites declared that Chernyshevsky's novel had swayed them to use terror, explaining that the date they had chosen for their attempt on the czar was encoded in the novel.[13] The reference is to a passage in *What Is to Be Done?* where Rakhmetov vanishes, prompting the narrator to speculate that he might return in three years, when "it would be 'necessary'" and that then "he would be able to do more."[14] Since Chernyshevsky completed the novel on April 4, 1863, the revolutionaries got it into their heads that they were being called upon to assassinate the czar on April 4, 1866. Whether or not Chernyshevsky intended Rakhmetov to be understood as a "mortus," that is the meaning that Chernyshevsky's revolutionary readers gave to him. Karakozov's historian, Claudia Verhoeven, is very persuasive on this point:

> The Rakhmetov we know—the one the secondary literature generally characterizes as cold, cruel, and calculating: ascetic and austere; rational and regimented; utilitarian; and, finally, "Machiavellian"—this Rakhmetov only came into being after April 4. In short: what has always looked like the source for all of Russia's ruthless revolutionaries up to and including Lenin, Rakhmetov the "rigorist," only looks that way because he is seen through the filter based on the reactionary reception of Karakozov's political action.[15]

Being itself propaganda, *What Is to Be Done?* taught the Ishutinites that propaganda may exist in the traditional form of proclamations and in the symbolic form of "propaganda of the deed." Rakhmetov was preparing his body for an act of propaganda of the deed. In the lead-up to his attempt on the czar, Karakozov had disseminated a proclamation, "To My Friends the Workers," where he called peasant workers to open rebellion. In a letter to the governor of St. Petersburg, he had threatened to sacrifice his life in an attempt to assassinate the "evil czar." So much for traditional propaganda. Now Karakozov "transform[ed] his own death into the last possible act proper to the propagandist," "propaganda of the deed," and in his assassination attempt his sick body was "the word become flesh, act, and fact."[16]

This terrorist mode of behavior proved resilient. Twenty-five years later, in 1892, the Russian-born anarchist terrorist Alexander Berkman, who had immigrated to the United States in 1888, decided to make an example of the strike-busting industrialist Henry Clay Frick. Berkman's plan was to kill Frick and then himself in an act of "propaganda of the deed." Berkman went to Frick's office in New York City but could not reach him on his first attempt. He checked into a hotel under the pseudonym "Rakhmetov" and had better luck the next day. Bursting into Frick's office, "Rakhmetov" began firing a revolver at Frick's head. With two bullets in him, Frick jumped on Berkman and pummeled him, while the latter shanked him repeatedly in the leg with a sharpened metal file. Upon his arrest Berkman tried to commit suicide by means of a dynamite capsule but was stopped, much as Karakozov was prevented from taking poison and thus becoming a *mortus*. Frick was back at work within days. Berkman rotted in prison for fourteen years.

Sergei Nechaev, too, refashioned himself in Rakhmetov's image. His infamous manifesto, "The Catechism of a Revolutionary" (1869), describes a ruthless formula of asceticism that Nechaev applied to his own life and demanded of his comrades. The beginning of the "Catechism" sets the tone: "The revolutionary is a doomed man. He has no personal interests, no business affairs, no emotions, no attachments, no property, and no name. Everything in him is wholly absorbed in the single thought and the single passion for revolution."[17] Nechaev's revolutionary model is none other than Rakhmetov, who lives solely for the success of the revolutionary cause and nips a love affair in the bud, telling his paramour "that people like me do not have the right to tie another's fate to theirs. . . . I must suppress this love. Love for you would tie my hands."[18]

"The Catechism of a Revolutionary" also reeks with the revolutionary methodology of Nikolai Speshnev: infiltration, conspiracy, and blackmail. Nechaev had discovered the methods of secret societies while still an eighteen-year-old university student. His parents were born of serfs but had risen into the lower working class of tradesmen and shopkeepers (*meshchanstvo*), so Nechaev came by his hatred of slavery in a natural fashion.[19] In 1868 he enrolled in the University of St. Petersburg and fell in with the revolutionary students. With no knowledge of French (he later crammed French before fleeing to Europe) he nonetheless joined in discussions of François-Noël ("Gracchus") Babeuf's *Conspiracy of Equals*. Jacobinism, Blanquism, and the figure of Robespierre were inspirations for him.[20] It seems that Nechaev first found his way to the methods of secret societies through a native tradition: the history of Jacobin circles among Russian revolutionaries dating back to Pavel Pestel and to Nikolai Speshnev.[21] Pestel's activities in the Union of Salvation and other secret revolutionary societies after the Napoleonic Wars and leading up to the Decembrist Uprising of 1825 are notable for their use of conspiratorial methods. In 1816 Pestel rose to ascendancy in the Union of Salvation, which he renamed The Society of True and Loyal Sons of the Fatherland and reorganized, creating three rings: the Boyars (*boiare*), the Men (*muzhi*), and the Brothers (*brat'ia*). There was strict organizational discipline, with the Boyars giving orders to the outer rings, whose members did not know the goals of the inner ring. Pestel's goal of a constitutional monarchy was far too mild for Nechaev's taste, but his conspiratorial methods would have appealed.

Speshnev is much closer to Nechaev, not only in his methodology but also in his goals. Nechaev's revolutionary plan of the 1860s is none other than Speshnev's conspiratorial web of fives. The connecting link was Pyotr Tkachev, with whom Nechaev collaborated in the late 1860s, fomenting revolutionary activity among Russian students in St. Petersburg. Tkachev was a revolutionary critic whose ideas, like those of Nechaev, would influence Lenin. He had begun his writing career by publishing several articles about law in, of all places, the Dostoevsky brothers *Time* and *Epoch*. These mild articles may have been a cover for his more radical activities, for he remained ever a political extremist of the communist-Jacobin and Blanquist stripe. Tkachev's revolutionary activities continued throughout the 1860s despite multiple arrests and police searches. He thought it futile to wait for the peasants and working class to rise up on their own. The revolutionary vanguard, operating under the principles of central organization, strict discipline, speed, and decisiveness, would guide the majority, over which it must exercise absolute control. These extreme views and plans made Tkachev a natural ally of Nechaev. Tkachev had formed a revolutionary circle, which Nechaev joined and quickly came to dominate. It is here that Nechaev conceived his plan of organizing a revolutionary network of five-man cells. Tkachev had in his possession a copy of Speshnev's conspiratorial oath. There can be little doubt that Tkachev had shared the gist of Speshnev's methodology with Nechaev. In 1869, apparently in collaboration with Tkachev, Nechaev drafted a propaganda piece that would have pleased Speshnev in his revolutionary youth.[22]

"A Program of Revolutionary Actions" called for the creation of a large number of "revolutionary prototypes." These prototypes were to be used to communicate to the Russian populace the urgent need for the construction of a revolutionary organization. The "Program" demands public gatherings, "personal protests," the ubiquitous creation of revolutionary circles, and the propagation of proclamations. The revolutionary organization is described as decentralized, with a weakened center. This was supposed to incentivize agents and empower them to wreak havoc in provincial towns. In order to devote themselves to revolutionary activities, the agents, in imitation of Rakhmetov, were to give up their property, studies, family ties, but the authors hasten to qualify that the organization does not "demand total renunciation" of the same "since this would restrict without need or cause individual freedom, which is incompatible with an organization based upon rational principles."[23]

Of particular interest here are the opening words about the need for creating "revolutionary prototypes," by which, as we will see, he meant something like "superheroes of destruction," or more accurately "supervillains." In any case, more and more revolutionaries were finding in Chernyshevsky's fictional Rakhmetov a prototype and model. The "Program" reminds us that Speshnev, too, was a revolutionary prototype. Nechaev and Tkachev were doubtless engaged in Speshnevian mystification, according to the deceptive and manipulative rules of secret societies. It is inconceivable that a natural-born despot like Nechaev would in good faith promote an organization with a weakened center or allow anything but complete enslavement of his agents, but he was expedient and understood that he needed to enlist and encourage agents by giving them the illusion that they could act at their own initiative.

Soon after drafting the "Program," Nechaev began to put it into practice with the deceptiveness and ruthlessness consistent with his own Jacobin bent. At a gathering in January 1869 he persuaded ninety-seven students to sign a commitment to protest. The plan was for all of the signatories to arrive, probably at the Winter Palace, and to hand the petition to the czar himself. Should anybody refuse to appear at this protest, Nechaev threatened to reveal that person's identity and make him "answer for certain to the authorities."[24] There is evidence that he was planning on handing the names of those who refused to submit to him to the Third Department. It is likely that by these means Nechaev intended to manage his revolutionaries and send them off to provincial towns, as described in the "Program": to recruit, to implicate, to isolate, to radicalize, and to activate.

In January 1869, probably as a result of his activities involving student rallies and dubious petitions, Nechaev was ordered to appear before the authorities in St. Petersburg. Instead of doing so, he fled the city, but he performed another mystification on the way out, making it appear that he had been arrested by the secret police. He did indeed turn over to the police the names on the petition, but there is no record that he was actually under arrest. Even if he was it could not have been for long. On his last morning in St. Petersburg he handed over for safekeeping to Vera Zasulich a packet containing the names of hundreds of radicals. A couple of days later Zasulich received a letter from Nechaev. Nechaev had tried to make it look as if the student who delivered it to Zasulich had taken receipt of it directly from Nechaev at the very moment he was being carted off to prison. In the letter Nechaev wrote: "They are taking me to a fortress, which one I don't know. Tell this to the comrades. I hope to see them. Let our cause continue."[25] Inquiries were made with the police, who said they had not made the arrest. Naturally, the revolutionaries did not believe them, so Nechaev's ploy worked, and he achieved instant stardom in radical circles. While traveling to Moscow and Odessa in order to secure a fake passport for travel abroad, Nechaev had a friend spread the legend that he had escaped from the Peter and Paul Fortress, had been recaptured in Odessa, had again escaped, had trudged thirty miles by foot, had hitched rides in peasant ox carts, and so on and so on.[26] By the time Nechaev had left Russia for the first time, he was a revolutionary legend and the effective leader of the Russian revolutionary movement. Arriving in Geneva, Nechaev presented himself without any hesitation to Bakunin and Ogarev as an agent of a vast revolutionary network spanning the entire Russian Empire. He showed them phony letters and testimonials from all over Russia to support his wild claims.[27]

They believed him, especially Bakunin, who saw in Nechaev the next phase of the revolutionary movement that he himself had led in his youth. Bakunin forged an absurd document for Nechaev, identifying him as a representative of the Russian section of the "World Revolutionary Alliance." This paper bore Bakunin's signature and the seal of the "European Revolutionary Alliance." Now Nechaev belonged to two vast, powerful revolutionary networks, neither of which existed. Bakunin and Ogarev also gave Nechaev access to a fund left in their and Herzen's hands by a Russian revolutionary utopianist named Pavel Bakhmetev, who has been identified as a possible prototype for Rakhmetov. Nechaev used the money to fund a propaganda blitz that saw the publication abroad and dissemination in Russia of a flurry of proclamations. Herzen remained distrustful of Nechaev and urged Bakunin and Ogarev not to associate themselves too closely with him and to shun his "bloodthirsty" rhetoric, but he could not stop them from letting Nechaev tap the fund. Bakunin referred to Nechaev as "my boy" and "tiger cub." Herzen called him "a reptile."[28] Ogarev rededicated a poem titled "The Student" to Nechaev; Ogarev had originally dedicated it to his friend Sergei Astrakov, but Astrakov had died and could not object. "The Student," which was disseminated in a special proclamation, tells the story of a poverty-stricken young man who devoted his entire life to the emancipation of the people. For his noble struggle the "student" is hounded by the czarist regime, and, after a life of great hardship and wanderings, exiled to Siberia, where he eventually dies a martyr for the people and for the revolution. In a letter to Ogarev Herzen sardonically noted that he had "buried Nechaev alive."[29]

"The Student" is a platitude, but, like Bakunin's seal, it bolstered Nechaev's revolutionary credentials and put the nimbus of noble suffering around his head. Bakunin's reputation by contrast was irreparably damaged by his close collaboration with Nechaev. Because of his conspiratorial activities with Nechaev, Bakunin was banned from the First International in 1872, where Karl Marx roundly condemned "Nechaevism." Nechaev, while initially impressed by Bakunin, soon assumed a patronizing and overbearing air with him, attempting to press him into service as useful material for his revolutionary program. The deluded Bakunin and Ogarev went along with this humiliating usurpation, joining Nechaev in a collaborative proclamation-writing campaign. The Nechaev-Bakunin-Ogarev collaboration released a torrent of proclamations, written in Geneva, mailed from a dozen or so cities in Europe, and distributed back in Russia.

Bakunin had earlier met Speshnev in Siberia, where the latter had impressed him so much that he praised him in a letter to

Herzen. It is very likely that Bakunin spoke to Nechaev of Speshnev during their meetings in Geneva.[30] Nechaev, we recall, almost certainly knew about Speshnev's revolutionary schemes through Tkachev. Impressed as he had been with Speshnev, Bakunin did not approve of his Jacobin-Blanquist tendencies, and he tried to correct the same conspiratorial methodology in Nechaev by emphatically declaring in his proclamations that uprisings must occur at the initiative of the Russian people and that it was the people who should retain political power in the new order. Bakunin called the Russian people to a general insurrection and argued that Russia's violent common criminals should lead the revolt. Nechaev struck back by announcing in his proclamation that he was "severing ties with all political émigrés who do not want to return to the homeland" and fight alongside the domestic revolutionaries.[31] Nechaev demanded action, terrorism to be precise:

> Not recognizing any kind of activity other than the act of annihilation, we agree that the forms in which this activity can appear are extremely varied. Poison, knife, noose, etc.! . . . . Let all healthy young persons take up without hesitation this sacred cause of annihilation of evil, of purification and enlightenment of the Russian Land by fire and sword.[32]

He lashed out viciously against Herzen, Ogarev, and Bakunin, calling their phrase mongering about a utopian socialist future a dangerous distraction from the immediate necessity of destruction. Vague calls to arms not immediately followed by bloody proof of commitment were nothing more than "mental onanism."[33] It is amusing to imagine that Nechaev wrote these words dripping with venom while sitting across the table from Bakunin and Ogarev, who were busy writing proclamations of their own.

What emerged from this storm of activity were three proclamations written by Ogarev, two by Bakunin, and three by Nechaev, including the first of his series, "The People's Reprisal" (*Narodnaia rasprava*). Nechaev's "People's Reprisal" became the most infamous of all. In it he called for the assassination of high-ranking military officers, greedy magnates of commerce, and writers who apologized for the government. He described the need for an alphabetized list of such targets and in fact went to the trouble of creating the awful list—a small notebook containing hundreds of names of people he intended to destroy. And finally, Nechaev used this proclamation to break with Bakunin, whom Nechaev did not name, but whose proclamation "The People's Task" (*Narodnoe delo*) he criticized for being too pretty, moderate, and abstract—none of which prevented Nechaev from adopting Bakunin's entire program. Nechaev pretended ignorance of the fact that Bakunin was the author of "The People's Task" and created the appearance that his own "People's Reprisal" was written in St. Petersburg and Moscow, though it was in fact written in Geneva.[34]

While collaborating with Ogarev and Bakunin in the composition of the proclamations, Nechaev sent some very poorly encoded letters and telegrams back to his co-conspirators in Russia, compromising them with the secret police, who of course read all of his correspondences. As a result of his sloppiness, intentional or unintentional, fourteen people were arrested, including his sister Anna Nechaev, Vera Zasulich, and her sister.[35] Soon Tkachev, too, was arrested. The incipient revolutionary organization that Nechaev had helped create was now in shambles, and it was mostly Nechaev's own doing. When Nechaev returned to Russia in August 1869 there was nobody left to rival him as leader of the revolutionary movement.

Returning to his native land, Nechaev smuggled in the most outrageous proclamation of all, "Catechism of a Revolutionary." The only surviving copy does not bear the title "Catechism of a Revolutionary," but it so clearly answers the call from the "Program of Revolutionary Actions" that everybody immediately began calling it the "Catechism of a Revolutionary."[36] Its authorship has not been definitively proven. There are Bakunian passages about enlisting Russian "brigands" to the revolutionary cause, and Bakuninian elegance in much of the phrasing, but the brutality of the call to terror, the disregard for people's secrets, dignity, independence, and even life all bear the mark of Nechaev. It was written in Geneva in 1869, encoded, probably by Nechaev, seized in 1870 by the police in the home of Pyotr Uspensky, who helped the police break the code, and read aloud at Nechaev's trial in 1873. The "Catechism" is the final evolution of a series of programs that starts with Speshnev's "Oath" and becomes progressively more ruthless and bloody with Zaichnevsky's proclamation, "Young Russia," and the conspiratorial and terroristic dictates of Ishutin's Hell. It also supplies the cruel secret methodology to the misleadingly liberal agenda of Nechaev and Tkachev's "Program of Revolutionary Actions," to whose timeline it attempts to adhere. The "Catechism" draws its violent efficacy as much from a relentless economy of words as from the bloodlust of its content.

In 1500 words, divided into twenty-six paragraphs, the "Catechism" describes the revolutionary as "a doomed man." He is without property, without profession, without feelings, without friends. He has cut himself off from the civil order, from the world of education, from the sciences, from conventional morality, from all human society. His only passion is hatred of the existing order and the only science he practices is the merciless science of destruction. But even the passion of revolution he pursues with cold calculation. To this end he devotes the entirety of his energy and his full life force. He is prepared to sacrifice his freedom and his life for the cause and to endure any torture. He has already given up friends, family, love, and honor. He is immune to romanticism, sensitivity, and enthusiasm. His only satisfaction is the success of the revolution. Up to this point he looks very much like Rakhmetov. Now Nechaev divides revolutionaries into a hierarchy consisting of a first rank of fully initiated fighters and then a second rank of incompletely indoctrinated revolutionaries, then a third rank, and so on. The first-rank revolutionary trusts and confides only in other first rankers. As for those from the second rank, third rank, and so on, the first-ranker is to regard them as "part of the revolutionary capital placed at his disposal." He is to spend this capital economically, but spend it he must. The revolutionary must infiltrate all spheres of the world he aims to destroy: government service, education, the merchant class, the church, the homes of noblemen, the military, literature, the Third Department, and even the czar's palace. If his hand trembles when it is time to obliterate any of this, he is not a real revolutionary.

In the "Catechism" one sees a bureaucrat's absurd passion for categorization and regulation. All society is divided into six categories: the first is everybody condemned by the revolution to die; the "Catechism" suggests compiling a long list of these wretches. The second category consists of those to whom the revolutionary cause temporarily grants life in order that they bring the people to the brink of revolt "by means of a series of monstrous actions." To the third category belong "high-placed cattle or individuals, who are undistinguished either by intelligence or energy, but who exercise wealth, connections, influence or power thanks to their position." These are to be compromised, extorted, blackmailed, and otherwise enslaved, so that their wealth and influence may help bring about various revolutionary actions. The fourth category: vain and liberal government officials. The revolutionary is to pretend to conspire with these fools, presumably in following programs of moderate reform, while culling their secrets in order to leave them hopelessly compromised, thereby eventually compelling them to muck things up in the various government bureaus. The fifth category (to which Herzen, Ogarev, and Bakunin obviously belonged) consists of the "doctrinaires, revolutionaries and conspirators" of idle circles where nothing but talk happens. These theoreticians of revolution must be "prodded and dragged into difficult activities, the consequence of which will be the complete disappearance of the great majority of them and the authentic revolutionary rebirth of a small number of them." The final category is women, whom the "Catechism" goes on to subcategorize as expendable fodder, female comrades, and so on.[37]

There is no need to elaborate these organizational niceties any further; I do, however, want to pause to point out Nechaev's jarringly different tone when he writes of women. In what might seem a brief stylistic burst of Chernshevskian sentimentality, the "Catechism" refers to fully initiated women revolutionaries as a "precious treasure" to their male comrades. This was no momentary lapse. Nechaev seemed unable to maintain proper comradely relations with women. He attempted unsuccessfully to court Vera Zasulich and Natalie Herzen (Herzen's daughter) and with varying success many others. Later, in prison, in imitation of Chernyshevsky, no doubt, he worked on a novel called *Georgette*, which has not survived. According to a report by a prison inspector, Nechaev's hero in the novel, a revolutionary, is denied satisfaction of his sexual urges by the heroine until his revolutionary efforts bear fruit. Meanwhile he must be content to exhaust his lust with the utterly debauched women of the aristocracy.[38] This clumsy, infantile behavior contradicts the cold calculations, unerring organizational skills, and precisely plotted acts of ruthless destruction demanded by Nechaev's proclamations, and it would soon prove Nechaev's undoing.

In the same booklet with this "Catechism" Nechaev published two other documents that laid out the system of organization that the revolutionary movement was to take in Russia. "The General Rules of the Organization" and "The General Rules of the Network for the Sections" call for an original terrorist—Nechaev, say—to create a primary cell of five members. Each member except the founder of the cell would himself recruit four members to form four secondary quintets, and each of the four new members of each secondary cell would form their own tertiary cells, and so on, very much along the lines of Speshnev's system. And as with Speshnev's revolutionary organization, Nechaev's "People's Reprisal" was organized according to the principles of secrecy, deception, and subordination to a center. Each cell took orders from the cell above it and issued them to the cell below. A cell might, but need not, share information with the cell below it, but it must pass information up to the cell above it. All members understood that they could be sacrificed for the good of the cause. These documents refer vaguely to a "Committee" that has authority over the entire system. There was no Committee, especially as Nechaev had already fatally compromised his collaborators in Russia: there was only Nechaev himself.[39]

Sneaking back to Moscow in the fall of 1869, Nechaev immediately began to organize the People's Reprisal according to the system of interlinking cells. He recruited the founding cell from a circle of students at the Petrov Agricultural Academy in Moscow. Nikolai Dolgov (who would later conspire with Lenin), Aleksei Kuznetsov, Fyodor Ripman, and Ivan Ivanov were idealistic students who taught peasants to read in their spare time and who planned, upon graduation, to start up a commune. Joining up with Nechaev, they became the first quintet. According to Nechaev's organizational rules, each of the four new members was to recruit four members of his own to form four secondary cells. The recruitment did not proceed smoothly. Some members were better recruiters than others, so that one of them barely managed to sign on three new members with the help of Nechaev, while another ended up with five when two brothers suddenly joined together. The execution of Nechaev's plan for an infinitely expanding web of cells went as far as a tertiary level of cells, but there it stopped. According to the "Program of Revolutionary Actions," there was supposed to be a revolt in February 1870. The revolutionaries were to meet in October 1869 and agree upon a common set of rules and principles after which the organization would begin "systematic revolutionary activity embracing all of Russia."[40] But the implementation of Nechaev's fantastic scheme for revolution was derailed by the murder of Ivanov, and the murderer was none other than Nechaev.

Ivanov had stood out in this founding cell from the very beginning. He had taken part in the student demonstrations of March 1869 as a resolute and energetic activist. He had the reputation of being irritable, stubborn, and vain. There was also a rumor that he was endowed with great physical strength. He was the only member of the quintet who dared to disagree with Nechaev.[41] When this happened Nechaev would pretend to bring the dispute before the international council, which of course always decided in Nechaev's favor. Ivanov did not believe in this farce and refused to subordinate himself to Nechaev, as required by the organizational rules. Nechaev had given Ivanov instructions regarding the dispersal of propaganda at the university, and Ivanov had declined, so Nechaev and the others in the group gave Ivanov an ultimatum: either submit to Nechaev as his revolutionary superior or leave the People's Reprisal. Ivanov opted out.

Nechaev failed to describe to Ivanov the singular manner in which a member was permitted to leave the organization. He quickly persuaded the others that Ivanov might go to the police and report their activities. In a botched, gruesome, and evil farce, the essence of which Dostoevsky would capture in the chillingly comical murder scene of *The Devils*, Nechaev and the others lured Ivanov to a desolate grotto next to a frozen lake. When Ivanov arrived with his former co-conspirators to help them disinter a fictitious printing press, they led him into a dark cave where Nechaev was lurking, ready to pounce. Nechaev tried to grab and strangle Ivanov but in the dark seized another member of the group, who began yelping in protest. Ivanov bolted for the entrance but was recaptured by other cell members. Only Nechaev proved capable of decisive action, and, filthily cursing the others, he knocked Ivanov to the ground and commenced to strangle and bludgeon him. The latter struggled ferociously and bit Nechaev's hands several times very badly. Nechaev finally fired a bullet into the back of Ivanov's head. They tied bricks to the body and dragged it out onto the ice, where they had prepared a hole. Nechaev accidentally knocked one of the others into the hole, and he had to be extricated before Ivanov could be sent to his cold, wet and very temporary grave. With characteristic lack of care, Nechaev left a watch on Ivanov's body, which displayed the exact time of the murder. He also tied the bricks incorrectly so that Ivanov's body rose to the surface, where it was detected several days later by a group of peasants. As if these were not enough, Nechaev also departed from the lake with Ivanov's hat upon his head and only later discovered that he had left his own hat at the scene of the crime.[42] In the aftermath, while the murderers were trying to clean up all of the blood and changing into dry clothes, Nechaev cocked and fired his pistol, barely missing Ivan Pryzhov, another member of the quintet. Nechaev claimed it was an accident caused by injuries to his hands, but then added, as if in jest—Pryzhov did not believe he was joking—that it would have been a good thing, because they could then have blamed the death of Ivanov on Pryzhov. None of the conspirators had acquitted himself professionally during the assassination, but Pryzhov had distinguished himself by cowardice, and the others had been forced to prevent him from carrying out a stupid plan to steel his nerves with vodka before the encounter with Ivanov. Nechaev embraced Pryzhov and left. As Philip Pomper, sums it up: "It had not been a neat job."[43] Leaving calamity and chaos in his wake as usual, Nechaev fled abroad to join Ogarev and Bakunin for a second time, abandoning his fellow conspirators to their doom at the hands of the police. His comrades were caught in several widening waves of arrests; dozens went to hard labor and exile, where many of them eventually died.

5

Fire in the minds of men

Dostoevsky's campaign against Chernyshevsky and his followers intensified in 1866. He was writing his first great novel, *Crime and Punishment*, for serial publication in *The Russian Herald* (*Russkii vestnik*). The protagonist, Rodion Raskolnikov, driven to murder by the logic of rational egoism in particular and of the Western Idea more generally, kills a pawnbroker, proposing to help himself to her wealth and later help society. Amusingly, he first confesses his crime in a tavern called "The Crystal Palace." Raskolnikov's foil in the novel is a scoundrel named Pyotr Luzhin, a lawyer and businessman who, with a cynical giggle, evokes rational egoism as the vindication of his rapacious pursuit of material gain. Dmitry Karakozov made his assassination attempt on Czar Alexander II in April 1866. The event caused the editor of *The Russian Herald*, Mikhail Katkov, to postpone publication of the next installment of the novel in order not to upset his readers, who were bound to associate Raskolnikov with Karakozov.[1] While it has been argued that the Karakozov Affair did in fact prompt Dostoevsky to give Raskolnikov a revolutionary shading in the second half of the novel, I think Karakozov came into notoriety too late to have served as Raskolnikov's prototype.[2] That said, Karakozovesque *mortuses* would show up later in Dostoevsky *Devils*.

While members of Chernyshevskian sewing communes were being arrested in St. Petersburg as accomplices in the Karakozov Affair, Dostoevsky finished *Crime and Punishment*, married his stenotypist, Anna Snitkina, and left Russia for a honeymoon in Germany. He had planned to stay for three months but wound up stuck in Germany and Switzerland for four years, as his considerable debts made repatriation perilous. It was in Western Europe that Dostoevsky wrote *The Idiot* (1869) and most of *The Devils* (1872). Living in Dresden in the fall of 1869, Dostoevsky pined for home and devoured Russian newspapers at the public library. The growing political ferment in Russia, especially at the universities, absorbed his attention. With strange clairvoyance, Dostoevsky foresaw trouble at the Petrovsky Agricultural Academy in Moscow, where his wife's younger brother Ivan Snitkin was studying. He invited his brother-in-law to stay with them in Dresden for a while, until things had settled down in Moscow. Arriving there, Snitkin told his hosts about seditious activities at the university, confirming Dostoevsky's fears. Snitkin spoke with admiration of a fellow student named Ivan Ivanov, who had first joined

Nechaev's revolutionary circle, The People's Reprisal, and later had a change of heart and quit. Dostoevsky decided that Ivan Ivanov was just what Russia needed. Dostoevsky himself had undergone a similar change of heart after his arrest for involvement in the Petrashevsky Affair. He settled on Ivanov as prototype for the hero of *The Devils*, which he was then composing. Soon Dostoevsky learned with dismay that Ivanov had been murdered by Nechaev.

Nechaev and the other "Nihilist" revolutionaries of the 1860s–1870s are Dostoevsky's most obvious quarry in *The Devils*, but he cast a wider net than that. The crown prince, Alexander Alexandrovich Romanov, had always followed Dostoevsky's works with great interest, and in early 1873, through his advisor Konstantin Pobedonostsev, he asked Dostoevsky to explain his view of *The Devils*. Dostoevsky replied that the purpose of *The Devils* was to find the origin of "monstrous phenomena" like the Nechaev Affair. "Such crimes," wrote Dostoevsky, "are a direct consequence of the age-old detachment of all enlightened Russians from the native and original principles of Russian life. Even the most talented representatives of our pseudo-European development have long since come to the conviction that it is absolutely criminal for us Russians to dream about our distinctiveness."[3] This letter to the future czar marks an important point in Dostoevsky's political evolution. His anger had now taken him deep into reactionary territory. In the future he would be tutor to the younger members of the royal family and confidant to the repressive Alexander III, to whom he sent an autographed copy of *The Devils*. (Nevertheless, as an ex-convict and former opponent of the czarist regime, Dostoevsky continued to be closely watched.)

When Nechaev butchered his new hero, Ivanov, Dostoevsky took it hard. He was inclined to pour out all of his hatred upon the demon-conspirators in his novel and fit Ivanov out with the halo of martyrdom. He wrote of his vitriol in a letter to the poet Apollon Maikov: "What I am writing now is something tendentious, I want to speak out as passionately as I can. All the Nihilists and Westerners will cry out that I am retrograde. To hell with them, I will speak my mind to the very last word" (April 6, 1870). At the same time he wrote in a letter to Strakhov (April 5, 1870), "I wish to speak out about several matters even though my artistry goes smash. What attracts me is what has piled up in my mind and heart; let it come to nothing more than a pamphlet, but I shall speak out."[4] In the end, Dostoevsky came out of the Nechaev ordeal with one of his funniest and nastiest novels. The "artistry," though badly dented, was not completely smashed.

The Devils connects the revolutionary movement of the 1860s to the liberalism of Dostoevsky's radical 1840s. In his letter to the heir apparent, he was quite clear on this point: "Our Belinskies and Granovskies would not believe, if they were told, that they are the direct fathers of the Nechaevites. This kinship and continuity of idea, descending from the fathers to the sons, is what I wished to express in my work."[5] Dostoevsky was certainly on a monster hunt as he wrote *The Devils*, and he identified Belinsky, along with Granovsky and Herzen, as the original progenitors of the nest of vampires. "I criticized Belinsky more as a phenomenon of Russian life than as a person: this was the most foul-smelling,

obtuse, and ignominious phenomenon of Russian life," he wrote
to Nikolai Strakhov (May 1871):

> If Belinsky, Granovsky, and all that trash were to take a look
> now, they would say: "No, that is not what we were dreaming
> of, that is a perversion; let us wait a bit, and the light will
> appear. Progress will ascend the throne, and humanity will
> build itself anew on sound principles and will be happy!" In
> no wise could they agree that once you have set off down that
> road, there is no place you can wind up but the Commune.[6]

Without Chernyshevsky there could have been no Nechaev.
Without Belinsky there could have been no Chernyshevsky.
We have seen how little that is truly new Chernyshevsky
added to Belinsky's final ideology, but Chernyshevsky's distinct
contribution to the revolutionary movement was to present
these ideas in a novel whose characters would be imitated in the
historical arena. And the imitators were quick to appear in rapid
succession: Ishutin, Karakozov, and Nechaev.

At the same time, Dostoevsky's own biography provides ample
motivation for his obsession with the Nechaevites, and, for all
his invective, his attitude toward the Nechaev Affair was bound
to be complicated. As he dissects the rational egoist motives
of his fictional murderer in *Crime and Punishment*, the author
maintains a cool distance, but with *The Devils* Dostoevsky tries
to enter into the plot, shaping his literary version of Ivan Ivanov,
the character Ivan Shatov, in his own image. Like Dostoevsky,
Shatov is awkward, blond, shaggy, broad-shouldered, constantly
scowling, gruff, and unfriendly despite an essentially good nature.

The novel's version of Nechaev, the conspiratorial devil Pyotr Verkhovensky, while most obviously a reflection of Nechaev, took on some of the features of Speshnev from Dostoevsky's days in the Petrashevsky circle. In a fascinating development several years later in his *Diary of a Writer,* Dostoevsky would go so far as to defend the devils of his eponymous novel, and remembering his "personal Mephistopheles," Speshnev, he confessed: "I probably could never have become Nechaev, but as for a *Nechaevite*, I cannot guarantee, perhaps I could have become one . . . in the days of my youth."[7]

The Devils diagnoses political chaos as evil spread through the inflammatory language of proclamations like Zaichnevsky's and Nechaev's; in fact, the murder plot of Dostoevsky's own political "pamphlet" is driven by a hidden printing press intended for the creation of revolutionary proclamations. The former nihilist Shatov takes the press, promising to use it for radical propaganda. After his change of heart, he buries it until it can be safely returned to his former revolutionary comrades. It is when he comes to unearth it—in effect to remove its demonic body from the sacred Russian soil—that the nihilist conspirators do him in. This scene takes on additional meaning when we consider that, like Shatov, Dostoevsky finally came back from Western Europe onto Russian soil in 1871, still at work on *The Devils*, to find his native land burning in a radical fire for which he felt himself partly responsible. But then the genre to which Dostoevsky attributes his novel—the "political pamphlet"—was a dubious sort of fire extinguisher. One of the central concerns in *The Devils* is how difficult it is to resist the temptation to imitate evil, to guard against being possessed by "other people's words"—a phrase coined by the novel's most eloquent hero, Stepan Verkhovensky. So we see Dostoevsky working against himself: his original intention was to write a novel of political propaganda, yet verbal contamination, as Dostoevsky saw it, was the very nature of the problem in Russia. As he wrote he sought a way out of this logical trap.

The Devils combines several subplots and often reads like a book in search of a hero. It begins and ends with the strange romance of Stepan Verkhovensky and Varvara Stavrogin. In his gallantly liberal youth Stepan had aspired to help transform Russia into a republic, but, for fear of reprisal, he never dared to express these desires except in the most abstract form—for instance, in some gently insinuating lectures on medieval history and also in a long allegorical poem. When nothing comes of his youthful dreams, he moves in with the Stavrogins and poses as a fallen hero for the rest of his life, fantasizing that he has been "exiled" to the provinces, and that he is under close observation by the authorities. Stepan is tutor and surrogate father to Varvara's son, Nikolai. In fact, as the best educated person in the provincial town, Stepan becomes intellectual father to all of the main characters, but, as he admits on his deathbed, all he ever taught them was lies. When it comes to his flesh-and-blood son Pyotr, any sense of fatherly duty is completely absent: he simply sends Pyotr away to be raised by distant relatives. The pedagogical and paternal neglect will come back to haunt Stepan, and send the whole town to rack and ruin.

In the drafts of the novel, Dostoevsky calls Stepan "Granovsky," a reference to Timofey Granovsky, a scholar who had, during the reign of Nikolai I, lectured on the idea of Europe's superiority to Russia. But there are more important prototypes. Herzen, who died in 1870, had come to personify the liberals of the 1840s, but he had been unceremoniously dumped by the young radicals of the 1860s. Chernyshevsky had chided him for the comfort that his great wealth afforded him. Nechaev, as we have seen, went so far as to threaten old relics like Herzen, unless they gave up their refined posturing for revolutionary action. Stepan echoes Herzen's yelps of protestations from the early 1860s, as the younger generation attempted to push him to the side and go beyond the limits of his daring.

In a dramatic scene that exemplifies the generational conflict, Chernyshevsky's novel *What Is to Be Done?* actually materializes upon Stepan's coffee table, "material proof" of the fruits of liberalism. As his rage at the revolutionaries builds into a crescendo, Stepan suddenly fixes his eyes upon the pernicious book. His son Pyotr is present throughout the scene, sitting insolently on the sofa with his feet tucked under him, taking up more room than filial respect requires. This allows Dostoevsky to strike out simultaneously against three generations of Western-looking reformers represented by the persons of Herzen, Chernyshevsky, and Nechaev. Needless to say, Stepan's own failings as Pyotr's biological father undercut his diatribe in some fatal way. Stepan has recently procured *What Is to Be Done?* and is "learning it by heart" with the sole purpose of discovering the radicals' "strategies and arguments from their own 'catechism.'"

At this point the word "catechism" was already inexorably linked with Nechaev, but Dostoevsky's task is to follow these links back to their point of origin. Stepan wishes to ready himself for a final battle with the radicals and nihilists and "defeat them in *her eyes*."[8]

Varvara Stavrogin had fallen in love with Stepan in their youth and tried to help him promote the liberal cause by founding a literary salon and a journal as platforms for his message. She became disillusioned with him, though, when she perceived that he would never really do anything except surrender to his foibles—principally, sloth, wine, wit, gossip, and cowardice—in a gradual decline. Add to that his dishonest condescension toward her as that necessary evil, the wealthy patroness, and—most unforgivably—a certain disdain for her feminine charms, and the whole situation becomes charged with disastrous potential. When Pyotr arrives and, after some fruitful snooping and spying *à la* Nechaev, reveals to Varvara Stepan's disloyalty to her, she tries, in an excess of wounded pride, to marry him off to her ward, Dasha. Dasha has had an affair with Nikolai, and Varvara would like to patch up Dasha's reputation and cover the trail. In short, two birds with one stone. Stepan, however, is too proud to accept a second-rate fate, which is the reason he had "spurned" the rich but plain Varvara in the first place. Unbeknownst to Stepan himself, he is madly in love with Varvara.

And now we can return to Stepan's parlor, where Chernyshevsky's hateful novel lies on the table. "O," remarks the narrator, "how that book tormented him! From time to time he would fling it down in despair and, jumping up, and begin to pace the room, almost in a frenzy."

"I agree that the author's fundamental idea is true. . . . But you know that only makes it more terrible! It's our own, our very own idea, ours and nobody else's. . . . Yes, and what on earth could they have possibly said about it that was new after us! But, my god, the way it's been expressed here, mutilated, muddled!" he exclaimed, rapping the book with his fingers. . . . "Educating yourself?" Pyotr Stepanovich sneered, taking the book from the table and reading its title. "You're long overdue. I'll bring you something even better if you like."[9]

It is characteristic of the generational strife Dostoevsky is depicting that Chernyshevsky was impatient with his spiritual teacher Herzen, whereas Herzen complained that his ideas were being dragged through the muck. For the next generation even *What Is to Be Done?* has become outdated and tame compared with the revolutionary propaganda of the late 1860s. Pyotr calls his father a "sponger," tells him that he has served in Varvara's household for two decades as a "lackey" and "fool," and admits with evil joy that he has shown her some terribly compromising letters that Stepan unwisely sent to him. In the letters Stepan complained to Pyotr that Varvara envied his talents, that she was exploiting him, and that he did not want to marry "someone else's sins."[10] Dostoevsky's point is that it is our own sins and not "someone else's" that will always come home to roost. Abandon your son to be raised by distant relatives and he will hate you. Betray your benefactress, and she will discover your treachery.

Spew phrases about the evils of tyranny, and you will awaken in the next generation a willingness to do something about it. The scene ends with Stepan putting a father's curse on the head of his child, even as the child, with malicious perspicuity, observes that, all the same, "there was a moment when she was ready to marry you."[11]

The elites of the town of N have organized a charity ball, and as the town's leading literary light, Stepan is to occupy a place of honor in the program, but Pyotr schemes with spectacular success to undermine the soirée and turn it to mayhem. The townsfolk come to the literary reading riled up over some revolutionary proclamations that have appeared in town and looking for trouble. The first sign of it arises during the farewell speech by the "great writer," Semyon Karmazinov, who precedes Stepan on stage.

In the person of "the great writer Karmazinov," Dostoevsky serves up Turgenev a plate of cold revenge for his cruel treatment of Dostoevsky during their youth, when they both belonged to Belinsky's circle. Karmazinov's expert manipulation of people, his haughty, precious manners, even his physical features make him easily recognizable; Turgenev did in fact recognize the caricature and complained bitterly. The satire aims mostly at Turgenev's writings of the 1860s. Turgenev's most famous novel, *Fathers and Sons*, written in 1862, had served as the immediate inspiration for *What Is to Be Done?* In it Turgenev had set up the whole paradigm of fathers and children for Russian literature: the fathers are liberals who retain their love for beauty, poetry, and Pushkin. The sons are materialists, represented by Turgenev's famous "nihilist" hero, Evgeny Bazarov, who recognizes only reason and science. Bazarov denies the existence of superstitions like love but nevertheless cannot help falling in love. This proves fatal to him. As Bazarov's star descends, his best friend and sidekick, Arkady Kirsanov, joins the "fathers," choosing beauty over materialism. *Fathers and Sons* is full of complexity and nuance, and it is difficult to grasp where precisely the author stands in this great struggle between old and new values. Chernyshevsky in his vastly inferior novel mercilessly obliterates any signs of Turgenevian equivocation. Here there is no nostalgia whatever for a pastoral Russia with its old values; Chernyshevsky is decisively in agreement with his nihilists. Lopukhov, Kirsanov, and Vera, armed with rational egoism, even get to experience the pleasures of love without falling, like Bazarov, into fatal contradictions.

If Dostoevsky shared one thing with Chernyshevsky it was his loathing for compromise and for moderate liberalism. With his character Karmazinov, Dostoevsky makes the point that Turgenev equivocated over Bazarov. In his writing as well as his life Turgenev curried favor with the socialists, and in his foreword to the 1869 edition of *Fathers and Sons*, even boasts that he shares almost all of Bazarov's convictions, coyly suggesting that he himself might be a "nihilist."[12] Dostoevsky's friend Strakhov seized upon Turgenev's scandalous "confession" and penned a sarcastic article, "Turgenev—a Nihilist! Turgenev shares the convictions of Bazarov!"[13] Turgenev's published identification with the nihilists and Strakhov's reply occurred just as Dostoevsky began work on *The Devils*, so it was inevitable that Turgenev become one of Dostoevsky's targets. Karmazinov actually goes so far as to ask Pyotr to tell him the date the revolution is to commence so that he might bail and cozily retire to his villa in Karlstruhe. The audience at the literary soirée greets Karmazinov's farewell to Russian literature, pompously entitled "Merci," with hoots of derision.

It is now that the unfortunate Stepan occupies the stage. Warmed up by Karmazinov's presumptions, the crowd grows ugly. As chaos breaks out, Stepan goes off-script and begins to scream out his artistic credo over the hoots and catcalls of an increasingly wild audience:

> The whole perplexity lies in just what is more beautiful: Shakespeare or boots, Raphael or petroleum? . . . And I proclaim that Shakespeare and Raphael are higher than the emancipation of the serfs, higher than nationality, higher than socialism, higher than the younger generation, higher than chemistry, higher than almost all mankind, for they are already the fruit, the real fruit of all mankind, and maybe the highest fruit there ever may be! A form of beauty already achieved, without which I might not even consent to live.[14]

Stepan is attacking the notion from Chernyshevsky's infamous master's thesis that "works of art are lower than beauty in the real world" or that the "imagination cannot conceive of anything better than an actual rose."[15] The radical critic Dmitry Pisarev had later expatiated on this idea, insisting that utility, not beauty, was the great criterion of art and criticizing Pushkin as an empty stylist.[16] For critics like Belinsky, Chernyshevsky, and

Pisarev, the utility of art was in its capacity to depict injustice, thereby inspiring revolutionary action. Putting together Stepan's final revelations about art, religion, and nationality, we arrive at Dostoevsky's central message: Russia has been possessed by the Western Idea but will soon be purged; after the aesthetic and ethical sickness passes, the intelligentsia will see again that God exists, that the peasants have preserved this truth in their religious practice, and that artistic beauty is the highest human achievement, because man is most like his creator when he creates beauty.

Meanwhile the town's factory workers are on strike, and fire breaks out. The scene harkens back to the fires in St. Petersburg, 1862. The governor, driven half-insane by the revolutionary mayhem, runs about the scene of destruction, declaring that "the fire is in the minds of people, not on the rooftops," and Dostoevsky's point could not be more clear.[17] Despite Stepan's pretty speechifying, it is precisely his liberalism that has caught fire in the minds of the young people and is merely waiting for the right moment to spread to the rooftops. At this moment a member of the audience at the literary ball heckles Stepan, pointing out that one of the chief arsonists and murderers, a certain Fedka the Convict, was once Stepan's serf, before Stepan lost him in a game of cards.[18] You cannot save Russia with phrase mongering about beauty.

Spurned by the townsfolk, unwilling to marry "somebody else's sins," Stepan "escapes," finally finding the courage to leave the Stavrogin estate, which, presumably, he should have done decades earlier. So begin his wanderings in the countryside in search of Russia. Stepan's lack of feeling for his native land is so complete that he can only bring himself to utter Russian proverbs in French translation. He does eventually discover "notre sainte Russie"[19] in the peasants and their traditional Christian beliefs, but in the process he proves himself to be physically unfit for such travels and catches cold. As illness and approaching death strip away all of the illusions of pride, he experiences a religious apocalypse and asks a peasant girl who has been traveling with him to read from the Gospels. He is interested in the chapter from Luke where Jesus drives a legion of devils from a possessed man, causing the demons to enter into a herd of swine, which go mad and drown themselves in a river. Stepan's interpretation of the passage gives the novel its title and one of its two epigraphs:

> You see, it's exactly like our Russia. These demons who come out of a sick man and enter into the swine—it's all the sores, all the miasmas, all the uncleanness, all the big and little demons piled up . . . in our Russia, for centuries, for centuries! . . . But a great will and a great thought will descend to her from on high, as upon that insane possessed man, and out will come all these demons. . . . And they will beg to enter into the swine. And perhaps they already have! It is us, us and them, and Petrushka. . . . and I, perhaps, first, at the head, and we will rush, insane and raging, from the cliff down into the sea, and all be drowned, and good riddance to us, because that's the most we're fit for. But the sick man will be healed and "sit at the feet of Jesus."[20]

After his fleeting moment of clarity, Stepan dies, almost happy, in the arms of his beloved Varvara.

Doing so he cedes the field to his former charge, Stavrogin. After a childhood under the tutelage of Stepan, who instills a love of everything noble, beautiful, and liberal in him, Stavrogin leaves his native town for a university education in St. Petersburg. Here he surrounds himself with criminals and radicals, gets into trouble with the law, and returns to his native town. Things go badly here too: he insults half of the local squires and must be sent abroad to avoid prosecution and to silence scandal. Somewhat in the manner of Bakunin, or perhaps of Nechaev (or even of Dostoevsky, who himself had been abroad for a few unhappy years by this time), Stavrogin spends several years in Western Europe, flirts with the Western Idea in various forms, thinks up some ideas of his own, and returns to his native town. The townsfolk watch him closely, enchanted by his aristocratic bearing but wary of new scandals.

All of the main characters, one after the other, male and female, eventually confess their adoration of Stavrogin.[21] Stavrogin replaces Stepan to become the ideological and spiritual teacher of the young generation. But in this novel pedagogy can only take the form of possession, conflagration, or contagion. The liberal virus Stavrogin has caught from Stepan becomes more serious with him, evolving into open revolt against God and his order. Stavrogin in turn infects Ivan Shatov, Alexei Kirillov, and Pyotr Verkhovensky. While abroad Stavrogin had planted the seeds of some new ideas in each of the three male characters, converting them into "maniacs." Each maniac expresses a certain aspect of the Western Idea. Emptied of ideological content, Stavrogin returns to Russia in search of a new idea. He is intent upon experiencing some sort of terrible suffering. The question is what form will his suffering take. Confessing his secret marriage to a lame madwoman would be a good start, but he lacks the courage. Allowing a man he has offended to kill him in a duel is another possibility, but his opponent muffs it, missing Stavrogin several times. Yet another path to suffering is an attempt to "attain god" "through the toil of the *muzhik.*"[22] In short, Dostoevsky's Soil Program as a way of becoming the Russian Christ. This is an idea that greatly interests Stavrogin, but he is too proud to act upon it. In the end Stavrogin does not do well in his quest for a cross. The Stavrogin plot deflates when he fails to become a convincing romantic hero, rejects political action, shrinks from religious regeneration, and hangs himself.

Stavrogin's legacy, then, is the philosophy he leaves to his disciples, Pyotr, Kirillov, and Shatov. His thoughts prove too "heavy" for them, and they spend the rest of their lives writhing under these ideas, as if "under a stone that has fallen on them and already half crushed them."[23] The idea Kirillov has taken from Stavrogin is that of the "man-god." Starting with the rationalistic principle that God does not exist except as "the pain of the fear of death," Stavrogin guides Kirillov to the conviction that if a person were to commit suicide with the goal of liberating humanity from this pain and fear, that person would himself become God. Kirillov is associated with Hell's original *mortus*, Dmitry Karakozov, in Dostoevsky's notes.[24] He is an atheist who reads the Book of Revelation every night, yearning for the end of history, and thus the end of pain. Karakozov's conversion to Russian Orthodoxy in the days before his hanging may have prompted this fundamental contradiction in Kirillov's world view. Let us examine the contradictions more closely: Kirillov will kill himself in order to deliver people from the pain of the fear of death; which is to say that he will kill himself to become humanity's savior; which is to say that he will kill himself to become God. But "becoming God" means one thing if God does not exist and something entirely different if God does exist. Kirillov has taken rational egoism to a conclusion that Chernyshevsky did not articulate, even if it is implicit in *What Is to Be Done?*: in re-fashioning the world into a utopia, Chernyshevsky's "new people" set themselves up as gods. Dostoevsky very likely intended the overly rational Kirillov as a parody of Chernyshevsky's own man-god, Rakhmetov. Stavrogin, too, viewed in this light, resembles Rakhmetov, particularly in his superhuman strength and highly developed rational faculty; also in his own desire to sacrifice himself. The historical precedent of Karakozov acts here to color the blank Rakhmetov as a *mortus*.

Unsurprisingly, since it originates with Stavrogin, the hyperrationalism we see in Kirillov is also present in Shatov, whom it leads to a different definition of God: "God is the synthetic personality of the entirety of the people."[25] All the same, Shatov has gone beyond Kirillov in his understanding of the dangers of excessive reliance upon logic:

> Socialism . . . has precisely declared . . . that it is an atheistic system and intends to establish itself upon the principles of

science and reason exclusively. In the life of nations reason and science have always . . . carried out an auxiliary function, a function of service. They will continue to do so until the end of the ages. Nations are formed and moved by a different power, which commands and rules, but the origin of which is unknown and inexplicable. This power is the power of the unquenchable desire to reach the end and simultaneously the power that refutes the end. This is the power of the ceaseless and tireless confirmation of one's existence and of the refutation of death. The spirit of life, as the Scriptures say, are "the rivers of living water," whose desiccation is threatened by the Apocalypse. The aesthetic principle, as the philosophers say, is the moral principle, making the identification. "The search for god," as I call it more simply. The goal of the whole people's movement, in any people and at each period of its existence, is solely the search for god, for its own god . . . and the belief in him as the only true god.[26]

Shatov reconfirms Dostoevsky's belief, as stated in *Notes from the Underground*, that logic is only one limited human faculty among many: "Never has reason been capable of defining evil and good or even of distinguishing evil from good, or even coming close. To the contrary, it has always confused the two in shameful, sorry fashion."

All of Dostoevsky's great novels are demonstrations of this idea: reason confounds the mind of the rationalist, causing him to commit horrifying, unnatural crimes. In *Crime and Punishment* Raskolnikov is seduced into murder by his reasoning faculty, but later drinks from the river of "living life" and is saved. Shatov is a further development of this mystical idea: each individual must draw upon the spiritual life of his people if he is to live fully. Shatov's understanding of ethics is much deeper than Raskolnikov's, and he is able to discern the snares of reason and science: "Science for its part has given only solutions employing fists. Pseudo-science especially has distinguished itself in this regard; pseudo-science, the most terrible scourge of humanity, worse than the plague, hunger and war. Pseudo-science is a despot, the like of which has never yet been seen. A despot with its own priests and slaves."[27] By "pseudo-science" Shatov and Dostoevsky undoubtedly mean positivism, utilitarianism, and socialism.

Since Shatov warns that the scope of logic is narrow, it is instructive to examine the most logical and rationalistic part of his tirade, which is undoubtedly his definition of God as the collective personality of the people. Shatov's belief is that at any given time in history one nation and one nation alone bears the true image of God. After inheriting Orthodoxy from the Byzantines, who had inherited it from the Romans, who had inherited it from Christ, Russians have become the "god-bearing" people, and so it is only Russia that can lead the world to salvation. Stavrogin, even though he is the original author of this idea, points out that it merely debases divinity into an attribute of the people—the idea of the god-man. Foaming at the mouth, Shatov shouts back that it is the other way around: he has raised the Russian people to the heights of the godhead. The problem with all of this is, once again, that Shatov—like Kirillov, like their guru, Stavrogin—is an atheist. "Do you believe in God or not?" Stavrogin asks Shatov. Panting, Shatov replies: "I believe in Russia, I believe in her Orthodoxy. . . . I believe in the body of Christ. . . . I believe that the Second Coming will occur in Russia. . . . I believe . . ." Stavrogin interrupts this odd profession of faith, pressing home the point, "But in god? In god?" Shatov's reply is laughable: "I . . . I will believe in god."[28] Like Stavrogin, Shatov does not believe in God, at least not for the moment, and his apotheosis of man—Russian man to be precise—resembles nothing so much as an ugly ultranationalist fantasy. At the heart of Kirillovism and Shatovism is megalomania: Kirillov wishes to become God; Shatov cannot endure the thought that his nation might not be God's chosen.

Pyotr, too, finds his motivation in egoism. The idea Pyotr has taken from Stavrogin is that of raw power. Owing something of himself to Byron's Manfred and Cain and also to their Russian heirs, Onegin and Pechorin, Stavrogin becomes bored by his own power over people. Pyotr, however, observes the slavish devotion Stavrogin awakens in almost everybody and covets that power for himself. In his notes about *The Devils* Dostoevsky connects the character of Pyotr to Turgenev's Bazarov; to Khlestakov, the fast-talking impostor of Gogol's comic play, *The Inspector General*; and to Pechorin, Lermontov's tragic protagonist in the novel *Hero of Our Time*.[29] Later Dostoevsky shifted the Pechorin-like features to Stavrogin, leaving in Pyotr an unsettling combination of the historical Nechaev and fictional Khlestakov. In his final form, Pyotr retains no trace of Bazarov's intellectual integrity. Since he himself cuts an absurd and unattractive figure,

Pyotr decides that he will turn the tragic Stavrogin into his puppet. It is unclear whether Dostoevsky intends the reader to think that Pyotr's conspiratorial methods originated with Stavrogin. To the extent that Speshnev informed Stavrogin's image, this scenario is likely. As Pyotr attempts to turn espionage and blackmail against Stavrogin himself, one recalls Nechaev's schemes to control Bakunin.

Soon after his arrival Pyotr manages to insinuate himself into the three most powerful families in the Town of N: the Stavrogins, the Drozhdovs, and the Von Lembkes. The governess of the province, Yuliya von Lembke, deludes herself that she has taken Pyotr under her wing. She keeps trying to "surround herself" with the town's radical and wayward youth. Her plan is to influence these malcontents "through kindness" in order to "hold them back" and prevent them from leaping over the edge of a precipice.[30] The metaphor she chooses to express this folly fits well with Saint Luke's legion of devils, but what she fails to understand is that she herself is one of the liberalizing swine. The deluded Yuliya thinks she is the object of Pyotr's "fanatical devotion," but he is treacherously misleading her, worming his way into her confidence, spying, gathering information, compromising her and her husband Andrei von Lembke, the governor, whom Pyotr eventually succeeds in driving over the edge into sheer lunacy.

Pyotr's methods follow Nechaev's "Catechism" to perfection. His manipulation of Madame von Lembke follows Nechaev's instructions on how to exploit the liberals and sow unrest. And his game with Governor Von Lembke exemplifies how Nechaev proposed to use provocation. Pyotr suggests to Von Lembke that the only way to deal with the Sphigulin factory workers is violent repression: "But this has to be handled the old-fashioned way," says Pyotr, "Flog them all to a man and that will be the end of it."[31] In the "Catechism of a Revolutionary" Nechaev had instructed revolutionaries to goad the police to take reactionary measures, thereby pushing the people into violent reprisal. Like Nechaev, Pyotr tries to bedazzle his followers with his claims that he belongs to a global revolutionary network; meanwhile the revolutionary cell that he forms in the town of N is the first and only cell in this nonexistent web.

The socialists meet at Virginsky's house on the appropriately named Anthill Street. There Shigalyov, one of the socialist conspirators in Pyotr's quintet, presents his "system," which he claims to be the inevitable future of mankind. He has described this system in precise and exhaustive detail, so exhaustive, in fact, that its elaboration requires several thick, finely inscribed notebooks. His offer to read these awful notebooks to his fellow conspirators over the course of ten evenings provokes raucous laughter. More laughter is heard when Shigalyov admits that his system is unfinished and fatally compromised by an internal contradiction: in sad perplexity he informs the other radicals that "starting from the principle of unlimited freedom, I arrived at unlimited despotism." Nonetheless, he informs them, "besides my own solution to the equation of society there can be no other."[32] His solution? 10 percent of the population will lord it over the other 90 percent, who devolve into an obedient herd.

After the meeting, outside Virginsky's house on Anthill Street, Pyotr explains to Stavrogin that while Shigalyov is an idiot, his system is true. "Shigalyov," exclaims Pyotr, "has discovered 'equality.'" Note Pyotr's air quotes around "equality." Pyotr wants to persuade Stavrogin to join him in a revolution. After the upheaval, they will implement Shigalyov's system of "equality," which is Chernyshevsky's "Anthill"—the Aluminum Phalanstery:

> Shigalyov is a man of genius. Do you realize that he's a genius of Fourier's order, but bolder than Fourier, stronger than Fourier. I will manage him. He's discovered "equality"! . . . He's got good stuff in those notebooks. . . . He's got every member spying on every other member, each obligated to inform on the other. Each man belongs to all and all to each. All are slaves and equals in slavery. In extreme cases slander and murder, but the main thing is equality. The first order of business is lowering the level of education, science and talent. . . . Cicero will have his tongue cut out, Copernicus will have his eyes put out, Shakespeare will be stoned—that's Shigalyovism! Slaves must be equal: there has never been either freedom or equality without despotism, but in the herd there's bound to be equality, and that's Shigalyovism! Ha-ha-ha! You find this strange? I'm for Shigalyovism![33]

The part Pyotr has cooked up for Stavrogin is to pretend to be the true czar, thus inciting riots and revolution. Dostoevsky's artistic intuition told him that Nechaev's revolutionary scheme was a form of pretendership, and this actually turned out to be true, for a decade later, from his solitary confinement in the Peter and Paul Fortress, Nechaev hatched a plan to overthrow Alexander III by presenting himself to the people as the true czar and communicated this plot to co-conspirators outside the walls.[34]

If Pyotr personifies the despotism implied by Chernyshevsky's utopian equality, then Stavrogin, Kirillov, and Shatov are attempts at the opposing ideal of self-sacrifice as the ultimate expression of freedom. The fatal flaw in Shatov's ideology, recall, was the collision of his atheism and his fervent belief in the godhood of the Russian people. This contradiction dissolves, however, when his estranged wife returns to give birth to a child, whose father is Stavrogin. The birth of this child is also the rebirth of Shatov's belief in God. "There were two people, and suddenly a third person," he says in a transport of ecstasy, "a new spirit, complete, perfected, not the work of human hands. A new thought and a new love!"[35] And now his religious conversion occurs: "It seemed something was violently trembling in his head and all on its own, unwilled by him, pouring out of his soul." The key word in this key passage is "trembling," *shatalos'*, which also has the connotation of stumbling, faltering, quaking. This word is obviously the one that gives Shatov his name, so this is the passage that is meant to define and redeem him. His atheism trembles and gives way to belief in God.

And so Dostoevsky continues to preach his soil theory, which insists on the sacred nature of the Russian people, their moral superiority over all other peoples of the world. His main method is laughter, which is used to ridicule the Western Idea (materialism, socialism) and to create a diversion. Meanwhile, under the cover of all that mockery, a serious idea is smuggled in: God has chosen the Russian people to save the world. Shatov recants his atheism but not his ultranationalism and immediately thereafter receives his martyrdom.

As he worked on *The Devils* in 1871, the Franco–Prussian war ended, and the Paris Commune made its brief appearance. Dostoevsky mentioned it in a letter to Strakhov (May 30, 1871):

> But take a look at Paris, at the Commune. Can you, too, really be one of those who say that it again failed due to lack of people, circumstances, and so on? Throughout the entire nineteenth century that movement has . . . been dreaming of paradise on earth (beginning with the phalanstery). . . . In essence it is the same old Rousseau and the dream of re-creating the world through reason and experience (positivism). . . . They want happiness for man, and still stick with Rousseau's definition of "happiness," that is, a fantasy not even confirmed by any experience. The burning of Paris is a monstrosity: "It didn't work out, so the world must perish, for the Commune is higher than the happiness of the world and of France." But, you see, this bestial madness does not strike them (or many others) as a monstrosity but rather as something beautiful. And so the aesthetic idea in the new humanity has become muddled.[36]

Fourier's phalanstery, Auguste Comte's positivism, and the socialist utopias of Belinsky, Chernyshevsky, or Nechaev were fantastical rubbish to Dostoevsky. For all of their insistence upon science, the utopians' plans had never been tested in the laboratory, had never been experienced by any human being. In scientific terms, you could call them a hypothesis in the best case, but there was nothing scientific about them. All they really had was hubris: using reason to evolve new sciences, man would re-create the world as he wished.

Dostoevsky's sense in the letter to Strakhov that aesthetics had become muddled under socialist thinking is the very point that his character Stepan makes in his farewell speech at the ball. The formal ugliness in a work such as Chernyshevsky's *What Is to Be Done?* makes it a suitable vessel for an unlovely idea like rational egoism. Dostoevsky boldly tried to contain the ugliness and chaos within the stronger aesthetic order of his novel. *The Devils* attempts to neutralize Chernyshevsky's novel and the real-life Rakhmetovs it had spawned: Ishutin, Karakozov, Tkachev, and Nechaev. The idea is to contain the revolutionary chaos, by recapturing the real-life Rakhmetovs—Karakozov and Nechaev—and putting them back into literature, which is where they came from in the first place. But simultaneously Dostoevsky attempted to slip yet another utopian scheme into the reader's mind, and this opened the doors to chaos once again. Dostoevsky's Russian Idea is naïve, fantastical, and fanatical, perhaps as much so as the Western Idea. His strategy of fighting propaganda with propaganda, subversion with subversion, resulted in some very diverting, highly literary mudslinging, but in the fray Nechaev slipped away, and the Western Idea marched on.

6

Rakhmetov lives!

Herzen had been the check on Ogarev and Bakunin in their collaboration with Nechaev, and when Herzen died in January of 1870, they cast caution to the wind and joined forces with Nechaev. Bakunin positively rejoiced at the news of Nechaev's imminent return to Geneva. Upon his arrival the three of them launched a second wave of proclamations. "The Chief Foundations of the Social Structure of the Future" appeared in the second issue of *The People's Reprisal*. There and in his prison writings, Nechaev described the society that he intended to bring about after the obliteration of the czarist regime. In terms of repressive brutality it anticipates the novels of Zamyatin and Orwell. After destroying the old order, soaked in the blood of its victims, Nechaev's "Committee" would aggregate all power and wealth to itself and create a new order. Humanity would be organized into trade unions according to people's skills and proclivities. If you did not want to work, the committee would not compel you, but it would deny you shelter, food, tools, even the right to travel. Dissidents would quickly die off in a "soft kill." Elected representatives from each union would report to a regional "Office," which would facilitate the exchange of goods; regulate production and consumption; publish labor and production statistics; run dining halls, schools, dormitories, and hospitals; oversee construction and maintenance of infrastructure; and, of course, collectively raise the children. Mothers who wished to bring up their own children might apply to the Office for the right to do so, provided they had fulfilled their work quota. By means of a similar procedure scientists or artists might apply to the committee for the right to be excused from the labor norms in order to produce various works of genius.[1] Marriage would be banned as an oppressive relic, and people could come together and go their separate ways by mutual consent and under no contractual obligation. Nechaev's socialist utopia enforces just relations, levels all people, and fosters ideal conditions for personal development. In other words, Nechaev is essentially dictating happiness to the people—or death should they obstinately refuse to be happy. There is no need for police, courts, or prisons.

While tinged with Marxist ideas, this despotic rubbish horrified Marx himself, who called it "barracks communism." It is easy to see in Nechaev's horrifying vision of the future a further, more sinister, elaboration of Chernyshevsky's Fourierist fantasies from his novel of seven years before. Especially redolent of Chernyshevsky is Nechaev's reform of sexual and romantic relations. But unlike Chernyshevsky, Nechaev was a violent and angry man, and he turned Chernyshevsky's happy-go-lucky Crystal Palace into a miserable dungeon. The real reason Nechaev can dispose of the criminal and justice system is that his appalling "Committee" constitutes a police state that enforces a singular law: be productive and happy or die.

In his other proclamations, which were if possible even uglier, Nechaev created mutually exclusive mystifications. One proclamation, published in the deceased Herzen's *Bell* in the spring of 1870, describes a persecution fantasy in which Nechaev is arrested and deported to Siberia by three gendarmes. They beat him to death in an inn they commandeer in Perm and return to Russia with his bludgeoned, lifeless body. The vile head of the Third Department, informed of this bloodshed by telegram, leaps for joy, gruesomely licking his lips. But in a subsequent proclamation Nechaev is alive and well, delivered from the clutches of his captors. In a third proclamation Nechaev ascribes the murder of Ivanov to his refusal to serve the revolution and, with premature optimism, describes Russia as disintegrating into chaos. In a fourth proclamation he fantasizes aloud about his desire to become a martyr (i.e., *mortus*) for the revolution.[2]

Reading all of this contradictory, impossible information, the young Russian revolutionary German Lopatin concluded that the Nechaev affair (i.e., the murder of Ivanov) must also be a mystification. Lopatin conveyed his analysis to Marx and Engels, who agreed, concluding that Nechaev had turned out to be "simply a scoundrel."[3] Bakunin's close collaboration with Nechaev cost him dearly. The impoverished Bakunin had agreed to translate Marx's *Das Kapital* into Russian and had already received an advance of 300 rubles but could not stomach the work and had delayed shamelessly. He asked Nechaev to help him off the hook, and Nechaev, on behalf of the chimerical Office of Foreign Agents of the Russian Revolutionary Society The People's Reprisal, wrote an unbelievable extortion letter to the commissioner of the translation, N. N. Liubavin, calling him names ("kulak-bourgeois"), suggesting that Bakunin had better things to do with his time, and threatening Liubavin with physical harm, should he refuse to release Bakunin from his promise. Marx, who was coming down with a bad case of Russophobia, would use this letter two years later to eject Bakunin from the First International.[4]

Nechaev's machinations were not limited to extortion; he also spied, purloined letters, and infiltrated rival organizations. One little spree that was particularly damaging to his reputation—and by association to Bakunin's—was the Serebrennikov Affair. Nechaev sent his loyal henchman Vladimir Serbrennikov to infiltrate the Russian section of the First International, which was run by Nikolai Utin. Utin's group was vehemently opposed to the methods (extortion, terror, conspiracy, infiltration, and mystification) of Nechaev and Bakunin. Nechaev had Serebrennikov go to Utin, seeking refuge, claiming that Nechaev wanted him to infiltrate Utin's group. Astonishingly, this crude attempt at reverse psychology worked to perfection, and Serebrennikov served as secretary to the Russian section until Nechaev in his usual fashion began boasting about his successful espionage and blew Serebrennikov's cover.[5]

But Nechaev's entanglement of Natalie Herzen is his crowning achievement in terms of dragging people through the muck in the crass pursuit of power. Natalie was still in deep mourning for her father, when Nechaev enlisted Bakunin and

Ogarev (who regarded himself as her father) to recruit her into revolutionary work, embezzle her out of her inheritance, and revive Herzen's famous journal, *The Bell*, where they intended to publish just the sort of material that Herzen had strenuously opposed: incendiary, terroristic content in the style of Babeuf and Marat. Bakunin and Ogarev knew only too well how much Natalie's father had detested Nechaev and protested their involvement with him. This makes their willingness to accomplice themselves to Nechaev's schemes all the more deplorable. The whole dirty episode underscores the fact that even intelligent, gifted, and independent people proved pliant to Nechaev's will. Nechaev persuaded Natalie that the revolution depended upon her, since her father was gone and Ogarev was an unreliable drunkard. He pressed her into service by flattering her artistic talents, asking her to paint scenes that would incite anger against the upper classes. But she was repulsed by Nechaev's revelation that he intended to counterfeit money and engage in other illegal activities, and also by his clumsy attempts to make love to her, which culminated, as with Vera Zasulich, in a marriage proposal. Here one recalls that his socialist utopia had contempuously banished the marriage contract as a repressive relic of the old despotic order. Bakunin joined Nechaev in this effort to humiliate Natalie into acquiescence. They impressed upon her that she was an aristocratic vestige, a useless parasite and hanger-on, sponging off her brother's family, where she helped raise the children. They claimed that a woman of talent and conscience need not discard her life in this detestable manner, but should instead become strong and valuable by throwing herself into the cause of revolution. In her diaries, where much of this information is to be found, Natalie wrote that Bakunin and Nechaev nearly succeeded in making her lose her mind.[6]

Amazing to say, Nechaev was finally able to convince Natalie to recommence publication of *The Bell*, which he soon transformed into a more radical journal than Bakunin wanted (to say nothing of the journal's deceased founder). Ogarev and Nechaev agreed in principle that Jacobin conspiratorial methods were necessary for a successful revolution, and these methods were on display in the brief seven-issue Nechaevite run of *The Bell* in the spring of 1870. This is where Nechaev published the fantasy about his martyrdom at the hands of the police. At that moment the fantasy was about to be partially realized, because the Russian police had begun cooperating with their Swiss counterpoints to extradite Nechaev so he could stand trial in Russia. And even here Natalie helped Nechaev, hiding him, dressing him up as a woman, and bringing him to Lake Geneva for an attempted escape.[7]

Bakunin and Ogarev eventually realized that they had backed the wrong man. While supporting his erstwhile favorite publically, Bakunin finally understood that he had an obligation to try to protect his friends and relations against Nechaev and the "Jesuitical" methodology that Bakunin himself had sanctioned in "Catechism of a Revolutionary." In a letter of 1871 he warned a family with whom he had become friendly against receiving Nechaev:

> He has gradually succeeded in convincing himself that, to found a serious and indestructible organization, one must take

as a foundation the tactics of Machiavelli and totally adopt the system of the Jesuits—violence as the body, falsehood as the soul.

Truth, mutual confidence, serious and strict solidarity only exist among a dozen individuals who form the *sanctum sanctorum* of the Society. All the rest must serve as a blind instrument, and as exploitable material in the hands of the dozen who are really united. . . . Don't tell me that I exaggerate: all this has been amply unraveled and proven.[8]

As this letter suggests, even without his arrest in 1872, Nechaev's effectiveness as a revolutionary leader had been fatally damaged. His co-revolutionaries had cracked his system and discovered his lies. In 1870 Liubavin had informed Lopatin about Nechaev's use of extortion, and Lopatin was sufficiently diligent to make inquiries into Nechaev's activities in Russia. In a correspondence with Bakunin, Lopatin demonstrated that Nechaev's tales of his hair-raising escape and expansive revolutionary committee were all manufactured. Bakunin defended Nechaev almost to the end, trying to "save him" by making him renounce his Jacobin plotting. Nechaev was recalcitrant, and Bakunin finally broke with him in 1870.[9] In 1872, producing Nechaev's ill-starred death threat against the publisher of Bakunin's translation of *Das Kapital*, Marx had Bakunin excommunicated from the First International. Nechaevism was—for the moment—over. Without the support of Bakunin and Ogarev, shunned by most of the other revolutionaries, Nechaev had brought all of his own efforts to naught by dint of a series of fantastically irrational actions, wherein he vacillated between self-martyrdom and murderous tyranny. Again we see the irrationality and contradiction that underlie all attempts to deploy rational egoism.

It was actually in captivity that Nechaev immortalized his revolutionary credentials. At his trial, in Moscow in 1873 he refused to be represented by a lawyer, would not read the charges against him, and shouted in court that he did not recognize the authority of the court or regime as a whole. He had to be removed three times from the courtroom for disorderly conduct. He cried out that he was an émigré and that the murder of Ivanov had been a political, not criminal, act. He demanded that he be tried in an international court for political crimes. His jury of peers was unimpressed, and found him guilty in the murder of Ivanov. The judge sentenced him to twenty years of hard labor in the Siberian mines, to be followed by exile to Siberia for the rest of his life. He left enigmatically shouting, "Long live the Assembly of the Land" (*zemskii sobor*).[10] The czar, though, dictated a different sentence, fearing Nechaev would escape from Siberia, and had him thrown into permanent solitary confinement in the Peter and Paul Fortress in St. Petersburg. Even there, the indefatigable Nechaev could not stop. In strict and harsh confinement, he schemed, playing a double game by faking deference to the prison authorities while—successfully—converting the guards to the revolutionary cause through his old conspiratorial method, assigning each guard individual tasks, lying outrageously about the vast network of revolutionaries that they were joining, manipulating, threatening.

Almost a decade into his imprisonment, with the help of his guards and a secret code, he made contact with the leaders of the terrorist organization The People's Will, which had grown up out of the ashes of Herzen and Chernyshevsky's Land and Freedom. They were astonished to learn Nechaev was alive and not in Siberian exile. In code he wrote more proclamations, which The People's Will printed. He tried to persuade The People's Will that the success of the revolution required a revolutionary dictator, proposing—duplicitously, no doubt, for in his mind who but Nechaev himself could fill this role?—Andrei Zheliabov, one of the founders of The People's Will and a member of the executive committee. In a proclamation titled "After a Major Act of Terror—from the Public Safety Committee," Nechaev set forth the necessity for a secret revolutionary tribunal with horrifying powers. The tribunal would, in absentia, judge enemies or traitors of the revolution—who could be anybody—and either acquit them or condemn them to death. In the latter case, a militia of "revolutionary avengers" would arrest and publicly execute offenders. But, he writes, "in the majority of cases for speed and ease the carrying out of retribution will occur secretly, and all the signs of natural death will be arranged. . . . All advance notice and warning will be abolished, the tribunal will punish suddenly and unexpectedly."[11] In another proclamation he threatens peasants with eternal hell fire if they interfere with his undercover agents. In a third he informs priests that Czar Alexander III had been reduced by God to a state of idiocy and would soon re-institute serfdom, with Jews buying up the serfs in public markets.[12]

In 1881 Nechaev conspired with the Executive Committee of The People's Will to escape the fortress. He had communicated to them in code a plausible plan involving a ventilation pipe and the collusion of the guards, and he may well have succeeded, if not for the timing of "A Major Act of Terror" on the part of The People's Will. After the bloody assassination of Czar Alexander II in 1881, many members of The People's Will were arrested, and Nechaev's plan became unworkable. Within a year the authorities had decoded his communications to The People's Will, and he was put in Cell One, under conditions of pitiless austerity. With nothing but thin gruel to eat, no sunlight, nothing to read and nobody to ensnare, Nechaev soon became ill and died on November 21, 1882, on the thirteenth anniversary of the day he murdered Ivanov. Whether he died of scurvy and dropsy or took his own life is unknown.[13]

Nechaev's reckless haste, sloppiness, and ineptitude are characteristic of the entire history I am describing. Yet it was Nechaev's very incompetence that assured his deadly efficacy as a revolutionary. His slipshod manner of putting his methods into practice caused him to be immediately discovered as Ivanov's principal murderer, and then it was only a matter of time—about two and a half years—before the police, judge, and czar had arranged a martyr's death for him. Had Nechaev been neater, better organized, more careful, he would have had plenty of competition from revolutionaries opposed to his Jacobin-Blanquist program. He had become so tangled up in his own lies and threats that his terroristic methods were his undoing. But prison touched his image with the same aura of martyrdom that it had for Chernyshevsky, Speshnev, and, in fact, Dostoevsky. Curiously one of the books Nechaev was permitted to read during his imprisonment in 1873 was Dostoevsky's *Devils*.[14] History has not preserved an account of his reaction to his own immortalization in the image of Pyotr Verkhovensky, but it is fascinating to observe the adventures of the Russian revolutionary superman as he transitions from life (Speshnev) to literature (Rakhmetov) to life (Karakozov, Nechaev) to literature (Pyotr Verkhovensky) to life (Lenin), and on and on.

Nechaev had written in his "Program of Revolutionary Actions" of the need for revolutionary prototypes, and then he had discovered what was quite possibly the best way to become one. So what was the image Nechaev created of himself? Rakhmetovism was an essential component of it: rigorous austerity to the point of self-sacrifice. Nechaev startled and impressed fellow revolutionaries and would-be recruits by denying himself basic comforts and pleasures, instead expending his unbelievable, inexhaustible energy only upon revolutionary activities. He seemed to have created himself *ex nihilo*: a superhero or supervillain, but superhuman at any rate. Mystification was the second crucial component. He lied to everybody, exaggerated the size of his organization, invented secret international committees, and created legends about his travails. Terror is the final ingredient. People feared him, and with just cause. He carried a revolver and proved unhesitant to use it. He spied, pried, ferreted out information, compromised people, and ruthlessly subjugated them to his will. We have seen that he employed—albeit in slipshod fashion—the methods of French terror: secret societies, Jacobinism, Blanquism. Tiger cub or reptile, for years after the Nechaev affair young radicals poured over the stenotype chronicle of the Nechaev trial to learn the methods of terrorism; they made pilgrimages to the grotto where Nechaev had murdered Ivanov, as if it were some holy site; they reprinted his bloody proclamations as if disseminating holy scripture.[15] Among Nechaev's radical young admirers was Lenin.

Five years after Nechaev's death, Alexander Ulyanov co-organized the "Terrorist Fraction" of The People's Will and made an unsuccessful attempt on the life of Czar Alexander III. He was executed soon after, in May of 1887. That summer Alexander's younger brother Vladimir Ilyich Ulyanov, later known as Lenin, pored over Chernyshevsky's *What Is to Be Done?* It had been one of Alexander's favorite books, and Vladimir had read it before, but now he took it in with new eyes, reading it five times over. The meaning he now found in the book was so forceful that, in his words, it "utterly ploughed me under."[16] Lenin later recalled that *What Is to Be Done?* had awakened him, had taught him how to be a revolutionary, and had in fact "completely reshaped" him. One of the things Lenin treasured most in Chernyshevsky was his hatred of liberalism and compromise on the imperative of revolution:

> It is said that there are musicians with perfect pitch: one could say that there are also people with perfect revolutionary flair. Marx and Cherynyshevsky were such men. You can't find another Russian revolutionary who understood and condemned the cowardly, base, and perfidious nature of every kind of liberalism with such thoroughness, acumen, and force as Chernyshevsky did.[17]

The literary embodiment of this uncompromising revolutionary drive is Chernyshevsky's "rigorist," Rakhmetov, who is stoic, unbending, and strong. Lenin considered Chernyshevsky "not only an extraordinary revolutionary, a great scholar and a leading thinker but also a great artist, who had created unsurpassed images of authentic revolutionaries, courageous, fearless fighters, like Rakhmetov." "Now that," said Lenin, reminiscing about *What Is to Be Done?*, "is a literature which teaches, inspires."[18]

Joseph Frank perceptively commented that *What Is to Be Done?* "far more than Marx's *Capital*, supplied the emotional dynamic that eventually went [on] to make the Russian Revolution."[19] In Lenin's own words:

> Only Chernyshevsky had a real, overpowering influence on me before I got to know the works of Marx, Engles, and Plekhanov, and it started with *What Is to Be Done?* Chernyshevsky not only showed that every right-thinking and really honest man must be a revolutionary, but he also showed—and this is his greatest merit—what a revolutionary must be like, what his principles must be, how he must approach his aim, and what methods he should use to achieve it.[20]

The "Rakhmetovism" of which Plekhanov spoke was very strong with Lenin, who attempted to reprogram himself into one of Chernyshevsky's "new people." Of course, Lenin's exemplary new person was not Kirsanov or Lopukhov, but Rakhmetov, and not merely Rakhmetov, but Rakhmetov as impersonated by Russia's Jacobin revolutionaries, Karakozov, Tkachev, and Nechaev. Unlike these predecessors, however, Lenin was no martyr. And when his little sister told him about his brother's execution, Lenin replied, "We shall not take this road."[21] What Rakhmetov implied to Lenin was the ability to master himself with mercilessly strict revolutionary discipline, not in order to offer himself up as a "mortus" for the revolution but so that his hand would not tremble when it came time to spill blood. Orlando Figes convincingly connects the "strong puritanical streak" and "macho culture" which became behavioral norms in the early history of the Soviet Union to Lenin's imitation of Rakhmetov. Like his favorite literary hero, Lenin denied himself physical comforts, tamed and trained his flesh, tried to make himself hard and to harden himself to the sufferings of others. He did not smoke, hardly drank, and lifted weights. This Rakhmetov-inspired training program was mandatory preparation for the successful professional revolutionary. Stranger still it would carry over into his life as ruler of Russia, when, in 1918, he and his wife Nadezhda Krupskaya would choose to live in an austere room at the Smolny Institute in St. Petersburg, sleeping on bunks, washing in the morning with cold water, and calling one another "comrade" and "Ilyich."[22]

In 1888 the Ulyanovs resettled in Kazan, where Lenin frequented a Jacobin revolutionary circle that was attempting to revive The People's Will. When his mother found out about his revolutionary activities, the Ulyanovs moved again, this time to Samara, where Lenin immediately sought the company of Jacobins and terrorists, meeting with Nikolai Dolgov, who had been close with Nechaev in the 1860s.[23] According to Richard Pipes, while Lenin had become a kind of "transitional Marxist" by 1895 "at bottom, he was still an adherent of The People's Will of the kind his brother had been, combining with terror, conspiracy, and power seizure the Marxist beliefs in the inexorable force of economic progress and in the revolutionary hegemony of the proletariat."[24]

In 1902 in an open homage to his idol, Lenin titled his own programmatic book "What Is to Be Done?" In it Lenin argued that the working class will never come to socialism on its own but will inevitably require the guidance of an avant-garde of socialist intellectuals. This political impatience, this willingness to force history's hand, was characteristic of Lenin, and the legacy of Chernyshevsky. In 1904, shortly after the publication of Lenin's *What Is to Be Done?* the Menshevik revolutionary Nikolai Valentinov (born Volsky) fell into an argument with Lenin over the literary merits of Chernyshevsky's *What Is to Be Done?* To set the scene, a group of Russian revolutionaries were sitting in a café in Geneva laughing at books of questionable literary merit that had come to be undeservedly celebrated. Lenin was sitting with them, but maintained his silence. When Valentinov joined the other revolutionaries, he offered Chernyshevsky's novel as a prime example.

"One is amazed," I said, "how people could take any interest or pleasure in such a thing. It would be difficult to imagine anything more untalented, crude and, at the same time, pretentious. Most of the pages of this celebrated novel are written in unreadable language. Yet when someone told him that he lacked literary talent, Chernyshevsky answered arrogantly: 'I am no worse than those novelists who are considered great.'"

Up to this moment Lenin had been staring vacantly into space, taking no part in the conversation. But when he heard what I had just said, he sat up with such a start that the chair creaked under him. His face stiffened and he flushed round the cheek-bones—this always happened when he was angry.

"Do you realize what you are saying?" he hurled at me. "How could such a monstrous and absurd idea come into your mind—to describe as crude and untalented a work of Chernyshevsky. . . . I declare that it is impermissible to call *What Is to Be Done?* crude and untalented. Hundreds of people became revolutionaries under its influence. Could this have happened if Chernyshevsky had been untalented and crude? My brother, for example, was captivated by him, and so was I. *He utterly ploughed me under.* When did you read *What Is to Be Done?* It is no good reading it when one is still a greenhorn. Chernyshevsky's novel is too complex and full of ideas to be understood and appreciated at an early age. I myself started to read it when I was 14. I think this was a completely useless and superficial reading of the book. But, after the execution of my brother, I started to read it properly, as I knew that it had been one of his favorite books. I spend not days but several weeks reading it. Only then did I understand its depth. This novel provides inspiration for a lifetime: untalented books don't have such an influence."

"So," Gusev asked, "it was no accident that in 1902 you called your pamphlet 'What Is to Be Done?' "

"Is this so difficult to guess?" was Lenin's answer.[25]

Georgy Plekhanov, Lenin's onetime teacher and eventual rival, also admired Chernyshevsky, but not uncritically. Plekhanov traced the line of truth from Hegel to Feuerbach to Marx and pointed out that Chernyshevsky, as a "faithful follower of Feuerbach, allowed Feuerbachian errors to enter his philosophical system." Plekhanov attempted to correct these errors—something Lenin never dreamed of doing.[26] It was not the soundness of Chernyshevsky's philosophy that interested Lenin so much as Chernyshevsky's ability to radicalize Russians and enlist them in the revolutionary movement. Plekhanov criticized Lenin and the Bolsheviks roundly and persistently during the Russian revolts of 1905. He said that Lenin could not recognize the limits history put on revolution. For Plekhanov as a genuine Marxist, history required that agrarian Russia pass through a capitalist stage of development before it could conceivably enter into socialism. Lenin preferred to vault over capitalism and straight into utopia.

Lenin's *What Is to Be Done?* does not make for pleasant reading. It is full of ironic quotation marks, words italicized for special emphasis, and perpetual squabbling with ideological foes who should be (and had previously been) his allies. Lenin's prose style half-buries a despotic power lust in a medium of racking tedium with the result that the whole thing immediately bogs down in needless perplexity and awkwardness. According to the plausible mainstream reading of *What Is to Be Done?*, it is here "that Lenin first reveals himself and creates Bolshevism almost as a demiurge."[27] The workers, he says, will never ripen for revolution; "labor unionism" is the utmost of proletarian revolutionary ability. Marx himself admitted both revolutionary spontaneity and political organization as essential, but during the Paris Commune, for political reasons, defended the former to the exclusion of the latter.[28] Lenin, however, had better things to do than wait around for spontaneity: "The greater the spontaneous upsurge of the masses and the more widespread the movement, the more rapid, incomparably so, the demand for greater consciousness in the theoretical, political and organizational work of Social-Democracy."[29] Spontaneity is fine, but not without the communist party guiding and managing it at every turn. The obvious fact that spontaneity will by definition cease to exist once it falls into the hands of "organizers" Lenin pretends not to notice. Lenin goes so far as to say that it is the avant-garde's urgent duty to fight spontaneous movements arising from the workers.

> There is much talk of spontaneity. But the *spontaneous* development of the working-class movement leads to its subordination to bourgeois ideology, *to its development along the lines of the Credo programme;* for the spontaneous working-class movement is trade-unionism, is *Nur-Gewerkschaftlerei*, and trade unionism means the ideological enslavement of the workers by the bourgeoisie. Hence, our task, the task of Social-Democracy, is *to combat spontaneity, to divert* the working-class movement from this spontaneous, trade-unionist

striving to come under the wing of the bourgeoisie, and to bring it under the wing of revolutionary Social Democracy.[30]

The imperative to control and fight spontaneity implies a job vacancy, and those who fill the position will become the revolutionary avant-garde, exposers of the injustices of the autocratic state, agitators of the proletarian masses to revolution. "Our business as Social-Democratic publicists is to deepen, expand, and intensify political exposures and political agitation."[31] Lenin's explanation of why the working class will never achieve "political consciousness" (and revolt) without the guidance of the party is his mysterious claim that workers exist within the "sphere of relations between workers and employers," whereas political consciousness exists in another sphere, namely "the sphere of relationships of *all* classes and strata to the state and the government, the sphere of the interrelations between *all* classes."[32] But when Lenin lets us peek into this elite sphere (his own) where political consciousness resides, what we glimpse is mere terror: "The Social-Democrat's ideal should not be the trade union secretary, but *the tribune of the people*, who is able to react to every manifestation of tyranny and oppression, no matter where it appears, no matter what stratum or class of the people it affects."[33] Although Lenin declares that "agitation" and not terror is the appropriate tool of his party, any student of the French Revolution understands the meaning of "tribune of the people."

"Spontaneity" is not the only part of Marxism that Lenin attacks in *What Is to Be Done?* He also goes after Marx and

Engels' "theory of stages" as something hopelessly outdated and even politically insidious. More than anything Lenin's *What Is to Be Done?* betrays his attempt to consolidate control of the revolutionary movement. He aims scathing insults and sarcasm at other social democrats and attacks "freedom of criticism." Those, like Alexander Martynov, who insisted they were free to criticize Lenin's program are by definition "opportunists," "opposed" to the positions of true revolutionaries. The tyrannical urge in Lenin to shout down any opposition by means of generalization, simplification, or whatever device he deems expedient results in the heaping up of insults and slogans in place of logic. The "vanguard" of the revolution can only be the Social Democrat faction, with Lenin leading it: "It is not enough to call ourselves the 'vanguard,' the advanced contingent; we must act in such a way that all the other contingents recognize and are obliged to admit that we are marching in the vanguard."[34]

In an article of 1906 Plekhanov wrote, "Lenin from the very start was sooner a Blanquist than a Marxist."[35] Twelve years later Plekhanov saw the same Blanquism in Lenin's conduct during the revolution and tied it to Nechaev's methods:

The tactics of the Bolsheviks are the tactics of Bakunin, and in many cases simply the tactics of Nechaev. . . . . Nechaev spread the notion among the students that two million internationalists were prepared to rise up and support revolution in Russia. As the reader knows, among the working class today the equally baseless notion is being spread about the readiness of the Western European proletariat to support the Russian social revolution. It is the very same method, only applied on a much larger scale.[36]

Lenin himself sometimes identified his methods as those of the Jacobins. In his 1905 pamphlet "Two Tactics" Lenin wrote that if revolution proves possible "then we will make an end of czarism in the Jacobin style, or if you like in the 'plebeian style.'"[37]

The social democrats split into the Bolshevik and Menshevik factions at the Second Congress of the Russian Social Democratic Party in 1903. The new party that Lenin created in this decisive break with the old social democratic model was "hyper-centralised, confined to a few 'professional revolutionaries' recruited from among the intelligentsia, and dedicated to conspiracy" and in this sense it would later be viewed as "the ultimate source of Stalinism."[38] Trotsky initially sided with the Mensheviks against Lenin. In *One Step Forward, Two Steps Back: The Crisis in Our Party*, which Lenin wrote in order to justify his actions at the Second Congress, he had come out with the murderous formulation: "The Jacobin, indissolubly linked to the *organization* of the proletariat, *now conscious* of its class interests, is precisely the *social democratic revolutionary*."[39] In 1904 Trotsky published *Our Political Tasks*, his reply to Lenin's *What Is to Be Done?* and *One Step Forward, Two Steps Back*. Portraying himself as equally horrified by Lenin's ideas and writing style, Trotsky wrote that Lenin's program was certain to lead to a bloody dictatorship akin to the Reign of Terror during the French Revolution. Trotsky boils the program of Lenin's *What Is to Be Done?* down to *"centralised, complex co-operation working conspiratorially for some political aim."* Trotsky sees in Lenin's formula an attempt to update Jacobinism by imbuing it with a proletarian revolutionary consciousness that had been lacking in Robespierre and the other mass murderers of the French Revolution, as if that would make genocide any more acceptable. Jacobinism, Trotsky argues, was a futile attempt to cut through logical contradictions with the blade of the guillotine. Most alarming to Trotsky was Lenin's relentless campaign against moderation: "among the Jacobins the dreadful accusation was moderation."[40] But, says Trotsky, there is something in the social democratic party that is at least as wicked as "moderation," and that is "opportunism": "to introduce the methods of the Jacobins into the class movement of the proletariat is and always will be the sign of the purest *opportunism*, sacrificing the historical interests of the proletariat for the fiction of a temporary benefit. In relation to the class struggle, which draws up its strength only as it develops, the guillotine seems as absurd as the consumers' co-operative."[41] Trotsky shows that Lenin, though he presented himself always as the enemy of moderation and liberalism, had himself embraced liberalism in its extreme state of Jacobinism. The Jacobins had tried to use the guillotine to hack off the contradiction that destroyed the French Revolution: "They wanted an egalitarian republic based on reason and equality. They wanted an egalitarian republic based on private property; a republic of reason and virtue in the framework of the exploitation of one class by another." The French Revolution failed, in Trotsky's analysis, because its leaders could not evolve beyond their bourgeois inclinations, and so it is with Lenin. The coup de grace is Trotsky's conflation of Robespierre and Lenin, whom he calls "Maximilien Lenin."[42] Trotsky differentiates the genuine Marxist from the opportunist by contrasting the Marxist's optimism about the eventual "growth" and "evolution" of the proletariat's revolutionary consciousness with the Jacobin opportunist's pessimism and distrust: "*Our attitude towards the elemental social forces, and therefore towards the future, is one of revolutionary confidence.* For the Jacobins, these forces were rightly suspect because they also engendered the formation of the proletariat into a class." In other words, the last thing Lenin wants is for the working class to attain political enlightenment, because then it will not need a dictatorial avant-garde.

Trotsky and Plekhanov lost, and Lenin won. The Red Terror ensued, and, just as Trotsky had predicted, it was worthy of "the Reign of Terror" during the French Revolution. But Rakhmetov was not the only thing Lenin had carried out of his reading of Chernyshevsky; he also flirted with Vera Pavlovna's utopian dreams. And so Lenin's seven-year reign was not merely a period of terror and civil war; it was also a time of broad utopian experimentation in the spirit of Chernyshevsky's novel. As Richard Stites writes, "Hardly a phase of utopianism and experiment in society was entered without a nod to Chernyshevsky, to Vera Pavlovna, to her glittering dreams. The novel was cited and quoted again and again. Science fiction novels, city planners, and people living in communes invoked or emulated *What Is to Be Done?*"[43] The dream goddess's final commandment to Vera Pavlovna, "Strive to attain [this future]; work for it; bring it closer; transfer everything you can from it into the present," was engraved on the walls of the Bolshoi Theater in Moscow.[44] All this Chernyshevskian experimentation subsided when Stalin consolidated power in the late 1920s, and it began to be clear that the model going forward was going to be terror, not utopia. Those Russians, like Nabokov and Ayn Rand, who were fortunate enough to escape the repression had the opportunity to interpret the legacy of Chernyshevsky from a safe distance. Nabokov's literary response to collectivism was an individualism that tried to cancel the curse of Chernyshevsky, from the Crystal Palace to the revolutionary terror. Ayn Rand also painted herself as a champion of individualism, but below this surface lurked the contradictions of the collective.

7

The vengeance of the muse

The Gift (1937), Vladimir Nabokov's last Russian novel, is his very deliberate farewell to Russian literature. Alexander Dolinin explains that Nabokov may have found the initial inspiration for *The Gift* in an article he had read in the Soviet press around the time of Chernyshevsky's centennial anniversary; the author of the article urged Soviet writers to compose novels in the form of "entertaining biographies" of figures like Chernyshevsky and Nekrasov.[1] Nabokov really did wind up writing an entertaining biography, but the Soviet author of the article in question would probably not have been amused. Nabokov wrote *The Gift* during his final years in Berlin, as he was beginning to transition into an American writer. Before leaving Russian letters, he was determined to perform the ritualistic execution of Chernyshevsky's cultural influence. With the precision of an entomologist—after all, unlike Chernyshevsky, Nabokov was sufficiently curious about the world to conduct a scientific study of it—Nabokov captured, neutered, and displayed his specimen. In doing so, he knew the wrath he would bring down on himself, because he understood the profundity of the Russian intelligentsia's continuing reverence for the martyred Chernyshevsky and his aesthetic that insisted a work of literature was as good as the brand of social reform it demanded. The perpetuation of this view of art was evident in the Soviet Union, where, by the mid-1930s, Chernyshevsky had already been officially adopted as a model for socialist realism, the only legal form of art starting in 1932. Oddly, the principle of the unassailability of Chernyshevsky also held among Russians living in immigration, even to the point of censorship. And so the émigré journal that published *The Gift, Sovremennye Zapiski*, suppressed Nabokov's fourth chapter, which is a biography of Chernyshevsky written by Fyodor Godunov-Cherdyntsev, the protagonist of Nabokov's novel. This real-life censorship was prefigured in the novel when Fyodor's publisher reads the Chernyshevsky biography and then refuses to print it, fulminating that "there are certain traditions of Russian public life which the honorable writer does not dare to subject to ridicule" and claiming that Chernyshevsky's "works and sufferings have given sustenance to millions of Russian intellectuals."[2] When Fyodor does publish his *Life of Chernyshevsky* with another firm it is viciously attacked in the Russian émigré press: "a pretty example," as Nabokov says in his Foreword to *The Gift*, "of life finding itself obliged to imitate the very art it condemns."[3]

Nabokov's novel expresses the monstrous tenacity of the aesthetic curse of Chernyshevsky through a reference to the *mortus*, which plays an important part in the revolutionary tradition I have been describing. Nabokov indicates this tradition by actually naming one of his characters "Mortus." Christopher Mortus is the pen name of a female Russian writer, who is apparently a composite of two of Nabokov's most ferocious critics of his Russian period, Georgy Adamovich and Zinaida Gippius. In the spirit of Chernyshevsky and of émigré writers like Adamovich and Gippius, Mortus demands of Russian literature not "melodious" and "dreamy visions," but, "human documents."[4] As we have seen, in the aftermath of Chernyshevsky's arrest, the *mortus* came to signify a real person who had decided to sacrifice his individuality and life in order to become an impersonation of Rakhmetov, a suicide terrorist. The *mortus*, then, voluntarily surrenders his humanity in order to become a literary symbol or, in Nabokov's amusing term, a "human document." This is very much to the point in *The Gift*, where Mortus will attempt to assassinate Fyodor's *Life of Chernyshevsky* for failing to be a "human document" but will instead murder her own literary reputation, like some muddle-headed Russian critics of the nineteenth century whose opinions are "like a fuse lit at the time" that "have now blown these critics to bits."[5] Mortus's "incurable eye illness" is related to Chernyshevsky's famous myopia: they share the same short-sighted view of art.[6]

Nabokov was extremely faithful to the historical sources, which he "digested" for months in preparation for *The Gift*, causing a bad case of "heartburn," as he joked in a letter.[7] But his Chernyshevsky is an exuberant transformation of history and only a "human document" in a satirical sense.[8] With his subject safely contained within the literary terrarium of this playful biography, Nabokov could indicate all of the mottled contradictions of Chernyshevsky's life and thought, starting with the fact that he was a materialist but did not know nature in the slightest and raised the blind worship of material things to a spiritual level. He dared to create art but did not bother in the least about artistic form. Whether it be a tedious, tendentious article he was assiduously translating from *The Times* or a novel of his own composition, Chernyshevsky's text was merely a jumble of words that served as a convenient concealment for whatever notion he was attempting to smuggle into his reader's brain. And so, writes Nabokov's character Fyodor, "Chernyshevski would pretend he was chattering about anything that came to mind, just for the sake of incoherent and vacant prattle—but suddenly, striped and spotted with words, dressed in verbal camouflage, the important idea he wished to convey would slip through."[9]

While Fyodor finds inspiration in the best stylists of the Russian tradition, his biography does not let classical Russian literature off the hook in some uncritical fashion. In contemplating the mystery of Chernyshevsky's literary success, Fyodor blames Russian letters for failing to dismiss *What Is to Be Done?* with a salutary laugh.

> The censorship permitted it to be published in *The Contemporary*, reckoning on the fact that a novel which was "something in the highest degree anti-artistic" would be

certain to overthrow Chernyshevski's authority, that he would simply be laughed at for it. . . . But nobody laughed. Not even the great Russian writers laughed. Even Herzen, who found it "vilely written," immediately qualified this with: "On the other hand there is much that is good and healthy." Still, he could not resist remarking that the novel ends not simply with a phalanstery but with "a phalanstery in a brothel."[10]

Fyodor shows the culpability of the aristocrats of Russian literature who abhorred Chernyshevsky for his uncouth style, saw the connection between low form and low content, but cravenly gave Chernyshevsky a pass:

> Leaning his elbow on the mantelpiece and fiddling with something, he would talk in a shrill, squeaky voice, but whenever his thoughts wandered, he would drawl and chew monotonously, with an abundance of "well's." He had a peculiar quiet chuckle (causing Leo Tolstoy to break into a sweat), but when he laughed out loud he went off into fits and roared deafeningly (at which Turgenev, hearing these roulades from afar, would take to his heels).[11]

While Nabokov's character Fyodor is technically the author of the *Life of Chernyshevsky*, this is one of those modernist novels where the protagonist is understood to be a portrait of the artist as a younger man. Fyodor's authorship passes through a poetry phase in Chapter 1, an autobiography phase (his literary treatment of his father's disappearance) in Chapter 2, and a biography phase (his Chernyshevsky book) in Chapter 4, before he decides to write a novel in the fifth and final chapter. The novel will be *The Gift* itself, a discovery that sends us back to the first page of the novel, which we must now re-read from an entirely new point of view. To thicken the plot, in Chapter 4 Fyodor constantly refers to Chernyshevsky's real-life biographers, among whom there is a "plant," a fabricated author named Strannolyubski (which translates into English as, of all things, Strangelove, as if in anticipation of the fact that Stanley Kubrick would be the first director to make a film of *Lolita*). To summarize, Nabokov invents Fyodor, who in turn invents a professional biographer, Strannolyubski, as his most consistent source and authority. This whimsical structure provides much amusement throughout Fyodor's biography, as Strannolyubski is constantly dealing his subject "strangely-loving" backhands of one kind or another, as when describing the appearance of an eagle in Chernyshevsky's yard during his Siberian exile: "'It had come to peck at his liver,' remarks Strannolyubski, 'but did not recognize Prometheus in him'."[12]

In writing his biography, Fyodor first of all supplies a corrective to Chernyshevsky's incorrigible writing style. The strategy upon which Fyodor settles is one that Nabokov himself favored in his novels and also, notably, in his autobiography, *Speak, Memory*: the elegant intertwining of thematic threads. The first theme in Fyodor's *Life of Chernyshevsky* is "Writing Exercises," which eventually leads to the penning of *What Is to Be Done?* in captivity. The second theme is "Angelic Clarity," which culminates in Chernyshevsky's martyrdom. The third theme is "Traveling," which anticipates his exile to Siberia and his return thence. The fourth theme is "Perpetual Motion," which begins with Chernyshevsky actually trying to build a perpetual motion machine in his youth in order to free humanity from manual labor. This theme ends with the deus ex machina of the muses, who punish Chernyshevsky by eventually turning *him* into a perpetual motion machine as he keeps translating volume after unwanted volume of Georg Weber's *Universal History* in order to make ends meet. Thus does Chernyshevsky outlive his own martyrdom and waste his final six years in forced labor even after his liberation from Siberia: "Chernyshevski's feverish work on huge masses of Weber (which turned his brain into a forced labor factory and represented in fact the greatest mockery of human thought) did not cover unlooked-for expenditures—and day after day dictating, dictating, dictating, he felt that he could not go on, could not go on turning world history into rubles."[13]

Strannolyubski delights in the notion that the gods punished Chernyshevsky by crowning every one of his endeavors with failure: for everything

> he was returned "a negative hundredfold". . . . For everything he was backkicked by his own dialectic, for everything the gods had their revenge on him: for his sober views on the unreal roses of poets, for doing good by means of novel writing, for his belief in knowledge—and what unexpected, what cunning forms this revenge assumed![14]

Developing this idea, Fyodor describes Chernyshevsky as that absurdity, a "myopic materialist"[15]—the very phrase that will undercut Fyodor's pernicious reviewer, Mortus, with the suggestion that she is but perpetuating Chernyshevsky's errors. Chernyshevsky could not see the material world, had not bothered to study it in the least, and yet had the audacity of presenting himself as its champion. He loved fine clothes, furniture, gadgets, and machines of all sorts, but he was dirty, sloppy, clumsy, and mechanically inept. As Fyodor sums it up, "His love for materiality was not reciprocated."[16]

> Look what a terrible abstraction resulted, in the final analysis, from "materialism"! Chernyshevski did not know the difference between a plow and the wooden *soha*; he confused beer with Madeira; he was unable to name a single wild flower except the wild rose; and it is characteristic that this deficiency of botanical knowledge was immediately made up by a "generalization" when he maintained with the conviction of an ignoramus that "they [the flowers of the Siberian taiga] are all just the same as those which bloom all over Russia!" There lurks a secret retribution in the fact that he who had constructed his philosophy on a basis of knowing the world was now placed, naked and alone, amidst the bewitched, strangely luxuriant, and still incompletely described nature of northeast Siberia: an elemental, mythological punishment which had not been taken into account by his human judges.[17]

With Nabokov good formal structure is a maze in which perniciously stupid ideas become lost, never to emerge again. Only ideas of permanent value will make it through to the other side. As an example of what can go wrong when writers place content before form, Fyodor cites Chernyshevsky's thoughts upon his arrival in St. Petersburg as a young man: "He particularly liked the orderly distribution of the water, the sensible canals: how nice when you can join this with that and that with this; and derive the idea of good from that of conjunction."[18] A system of canals may suggest to a wandering mind through the power of association the distribution of wealth in a communist economy, but the two systems are only connectable in a metaphor. Social reform dropped unchecked into a novel becomes crude propaganda, and the effects of propaganda may be anything but "good." Fyodor attributes the unwholesomeness of Chernyshevsky's ideas to their failure to break free from his flesh: "As often happens with unsound ideas which have not freed themselves of the flesh or have been overgrown by it, one can detect in the 'young scholar's' aesthetic notions his own physical style, the very sound of his shrill, didactic voice."[19]

Fyodor dwells upon Chernyshevsky's "infantile assessment of the most difficult moral questions." Rather than bothering with logical development, Chernyshevsky made gigantic leaps from idea to idea. Fyodor agrees with Chernyshevsky's "best biographer," Strannolyubski, who notes that, "passing scornful and impertinent judgment on Schopenhauer, under whose critical fingernail his own saltatory thinking would not have survived for a second, he [Chernyshevsky] recognized out of all former thinkers, by a strange association of ideas and according to his mistaken memories, only Spinoza and Aristotle, whom he imagined himself to be continuing."[20] Yet Chernyshevsky owed more to Platonic idealism than he did to Aristotelian realism.

In his naively uncritical fashion, Chernyshevsky accepted the socialist utopias of the day as the ideal political regime:

> The world of Fourier, the harmony of the twelve passions, the bliss of collective living, the rose-garlanded workmen—all this could not fail to please Chernyshevski, who was always looking for "coherency." Let us dream of the phalanstery living in a palace: 1,800 souls—and all happy! Music, flags, cakes. The world is run by mathematics and well run at that.[21]

The most profound irony is the fact that Chernyshevsky's pious thinking about materialism was itself a form of idealism:

> The idea that calculation is the foundation of every action (or heroic accomplishment) leads to absurdity: in itself calculation can be heroic! Anything which comes into the focus of human thinking is spiritualized. Thus the "calculation" of the materialists was ennobled; thus, for those in the know, matter turns into an incorporeal play of mysterious forces.[22]

Plekhanov recognized the idealism that sometimes slipped through into Chernyshevsky's thinking and attributed it to Chernyshevsky's uncritical acceptance of Feuerbach's defective brand of materialism.[23] Irina Paperno's analysis is quite sharp on this point: the essential part of reality as depicted in *What Is to Be Done?* is precisely that which may be transformed into something better. In other words, the defining, fundamental principle of reality in Chernyshevsky's novel is its idealistic transmutability.[24] How fitting then that Nabokov uses Fyodor's biography of Chernyshevsky as a lesson in how to transform a dreary "human document" into something transcendent.

Part of that feeling of transcendence comes from the idea of divine retribution. When the nihilist Bazarov denies love, denies friendship, denies anything but scientific truth and selfish fleshly desires, his downfall by means of unrequited love is tragic. When Chernyshevsky becomes unhappy in love, it is a farce. His wife Olga had warned him during his courtship that she did not love him. In their home, they play a humiliating parlor game in which he willingly acts out jealous scenes in the style of silly neoclassical comedies. Meanwhile, Olga deceives him energetically and often, sometimes in their own St. Petersburg apartment as he sits writing articles in his study. One assumes, reading *The Gift*, that she cheats on him because he has stuffed his head with silly preconceptions of what a woman should theoretically be, rather than bothering to inquire into what Olga Sokratovna actually is. Nabokov goes so far as to hypothesize that in cuckolding him Olga has become the muses' instrument of punishment for his crimes against Russian literature, specifically against Pushkin:

> We have in mind the following magic gamut of fate: in his Saratov diary Chernyshevski applied two lines from Pushkin's "Egyptian Nights" to his courtship, completely misquoting the second one, with a characteristic (for him who had no ear) distortion: "I [he] met the challenge of delight / As warfare's challenge met I'd have" (instead of "As he would meet in days of war / The challenge of a savage battle"). For this

"I'd have," fate—the ally of the muses (and herself an expert in conditional forms), took revenge on him—and with what refined stealth in the evolution of the punishment![25]

While it is unclear whether Chernyshevsky sired the children who bore his name, his descendants among the radical critics of the 1860s clearly carried his ideological DNA. And a seedy lot they were. Nikolai Dobrolyubov was the first to materialize. With his cheap parodies of Lermontov and his demands that literature become a means for social justice, he reduced "literature" to pamphleteering, that is to "zero."[26] And he was as unconstrained in his sex life as he was in his writings, as promiscuous as Chernyshevsky was chaste.

He had a German girl in Staraya Russa, a strong, onerous tie. From immoral visits to her, Chernyshevski held him back in the full sense of the word: for a long time they would wrestle, both of them limp, scrawny and sweaty—toppling all over the floor, colliding with the furniture—all the time silent, all you could hear was their wheezing; then, stumbling into one another, they would both search for their spectacles beneath the upturned chairs.[27]

Chernyshevsky's wife appeared soon on Dobrolyubov's list of conquests. "I know there is nothing to be gained here," Dobrolyubov wrote to a friend,

because not a single conversation goes by without her mentioning that although I am a good man, nevertheless I am too clumsy and almost repulsive. I understand that I should not try to gain anything anyway, since in any case I am fonder of Nikolay Gavrilovich than of her. But at the same time I am powerless to leave her alone."[28]

The double betrayal was painful to him, but Chernyshevsky soon forgave them both.

Let us warily turn to those of his children who bore Chernyshevsky's name, for here Nabokov has set a very devious trap. The Chernyshevskies had two sons, the younger, Mikhail, the good son, and the elder, Alexander, the prodigal one. Mikhail "was piously beginning his monumental edition of his late father's works, which he had practically brought to conclusion when he died, in 1924, surrounded by general esteem." But Alexander (or Sasha), a far more talented writer than his father, published a book called *Fantastic Tales* and "a collection of futile poems."[29]

> Created apparently out of everything that his father could not stand, Sasha, hardly out of his boyhood, developed a passion for everything that was weird, chimerical, and incomprehensible to his contemporaries—he lost himself in E. T. A. Hoffmann and Edgar Poe, was fascinated by pure mathematics, and a little later he was one of the first in Russia to appreciate the French "*poètes maudits*."[30]

Alexander's passion for pure mathematics enraged his father "as a manifestation of something nonutilitarian," and in his letters from Siberian exile Chernyshevsky abused poor Alexander for all of these eccentricities. This abuse was all the harder for Alexander to take because he suffered from a "mental ailment" that caused him to be placed repeatedly in a nursing-home: "He was afraid of slipping into a different dimension."[31]

This is a fateful phrase, as Alexander really did slip into another dimension. Starting off as his father's biological creation, he later became his biographer and thus re-creator. There were, according to Nabokov's scheme, two paths that were open to Alexander. The first: he could try to become his father's ideal literary son, somebody along the lines of Rakhmetov. And we do actually see him in 1875 ordering an eighteen-pound kettle bell and later joining a barge on the Volga. The next step would have been to begin hauling that barge from the shore in order to develop superhuman muscle strength, ideological "rigor," and revolutionary fervor. But no: instead, Alexander swerves from the path of the obedient son and "one sultry, oil-soaked, satanic noon, knocked the bookkeeper's cap off, threw the keys into the rainbow water, and went home to Astrakhan." He has opted for the second path, which would lead him out of his father's shadows and into a reality he could call his own. The second path will allow him to exact revenge upon the father who had called him "a big ludicrous freak" and an "eccentric pauper." Alexander (like Fyodor) begins his literary training by writing poetry, and what is worse (from his father's disapproving point of view) his poems "show a gleam of talent![32] In illustration of this last claim, Fyodor cites the following lines by Alexander:

> If life's hours appear to you bitter,
> Do not rail against life, for it's best
> To admit it's your fault you've been born with

An affectionate heart in your breast.
And if you do not wish to acknowledge
Even such a self-evident fault . . .[33]

Upon his final break with his nominal father, Alexander takes on a secret identity and pen name, becoming the selfsame biographer, "Strannolyubski," upon whom Fyodor most leans as a source of information on Chernyshevsky's life.

Petty, falsely funny misfortunes continued to spatter him. Thus we learn from a letter of his mother's (1888) that while "Sasha was pleased to go out for a stroll, the house in which he was living burned down," and everything that he possessed burned with it; and, by now utterly destitute, he moved to the country house of Strannolyubski (the critic's father?).[34]

The suggestion of a wonderful mystification arises: what if the Strannolyubski mentioned here, almost certainly "the critic's father," the one who lets Alexander live with him starting in 1888—what if he has adopted Alexander? The latter could obviously use a better father. Writing under the pen name "Strannolyubski," Alexander could avenge himself upon his father by becoming his biographer, the critic's critic, the creator of his earthly creator. To be sure, given Olga Sokratovna's amorous adventures, we cannot rule out the possibility that Strannolyubski of the country house is in fact Alexander's biological father. Returning to the first mention of Strannolyubski the critic, we see that he enters Fyodor's novel with the "happy phrase" that for everything Chernyshevsky did "he was returned 'a negative hundredfold.'"[35] This phrase establishes the theme of vengeance, a theme that implicates Alexander, who had strong motives for revenge against Chernyshevsky. The second mention of Strannolyubski adds another important clue: "Yes, he was always doing his utmost to turn his heart so that one side was reflected in the glass of reason, or, as his best biographer, Strannolyubski, puts it: 'He distilled his feelings in the alembics of logic'."[36] We find solid evidence that the biographer and the poet are one in a connection between this idea and Alexander's verses, "it's best / To admit it's your fault you've been born with / An affectionate heart in your breast."

The unmasking of Strannolyubski as Alexander Chernyshevsky helps solve the final mystery of Fyodor's *Life of Chernyshevsky*, the sonnet that encapsulates it as if in magical parentheses. The reader should be mystified by the conclusion of Fyodor's biography, where Fyodor cites "in full" a "mediocre but curious sonnet":

> What will it say, your far descendant's voice—
> Lauding your life or blasting it outright:
> That it was dreadful? That another might
> Have been less bitter? That it was your choice?
>
> That your high deed prevailed, and did ignite
> Your dry work with the poetry of Good,
> And crowned the white brow of chained martyrhood
> With a closed circle of ethereal light?[37]

The authorship of Alexander (Strannolyubski) is suggested in the use of the word "bitter," which appears in the first line of

Alexander's only other quoted poem, "If life's hours appear to you bitter." The image of Chernyshevsky's "far descendant" taking stock of his life again indicates Alexander, who, while nominally a very "near" descendant, has put distance between himself and his father by adopting another man's name and becoming his father's critic. The careful reader will notice that the "sonnet," "cited in full," contains only eight of the necessary fourteen lines. Taking the hint from the last line about a "closed circle of ethereal light," this attentive reader circles back to the very beginning of Fyodor's biography, and finds there the missing six lines, which supply the sonnet's conclusion:

> Alas! In vain historians pry and probe:
> The same wind blows, and in the same live robe
> Truth bends her head to fingers curved cupwise;
>
> And with a woman's smile and a child's care
> Examines something she is holding there
> Concealed by her own shoulder from our eyes.[38]

The first words following this epigraph to Fyodor's biography, technically the opening words of his book, are: "A sonnet, apparently barring the way, but perhaps, on the contrary, providing a secret link which would explain everything—if only man's mind could withstand that explanation."[39] The secret link is that Chernyshevsky's son has become his biographer. There is another link, a formal one, which bends the book into a magic circle, from last page to first, enclosing its subject within its prison in an attempt to distill his essence, his ideas, out of history and into literature. Truth is personified in this sonnet both as a woman and as a child. It wears "a woman's smile" presumably because Olga Sokratovna knows who Alexander's father really is, and it examines Chernyshevsky's life with "a child's care," because Alexander really did "care" about life, even about the life of his miserable father, Chernyshevsky.

Unlike Chernyshevsky, Alexander was fascinated by the world's mysteries, whether in the realm of nature, pure mathematics, or art. And he was enraged, amused, perplexed, and therefore sufficiently curious about the absurdly touching Chernyshevsky that he wrote a biography of him presumably under the pen name of his biological father. Such is the nature of the "strange love" the biographer feels for his subject. For all his "ludicrous and ghastly blunders," Chernyshevsky emerges as touchingly courageous in his "struggle with the governmental order of things."[40] Touching, too, is the depiction of the condition of mutual "silent treatment" that existed between Chernyshevsky and Marx. Marx, who could not stand Russians, wrote some derisive comments in the margins of Chernyshevsky's treatises on economics. Chernyshevsky, who could not stand Germans, "glanced through" but "didn't read" *Das Kapital*, instead ripping out its pages in order to make little ships with them, which he floated down the Vilyui River. This boat-launching orgy, according to Fyodor, was a sort of advance refutation by Chernyshevsky of a future biographer (Evgeny Lyatsky), who would compare the exiled Chernyshevsky to a man "watching from a deserted shore the passage of a gigantic ship (Marx's ship) on its way to discover new lands."[41] Describing Chernyshevsky's stubborn attempts to wrangle the Hegelian triad into something serviceable, Alexander (Strannolyubski) remarks,

> There lies concealed in the triad . . . a vague image of the circumference controlling all life of the mind, and the mind is confined inescapably within it. This is truth's merry-go-round, for truth is always round; consequently, in the development of life's forms a certain pardonable curvature is possible: the hump of truth; but no more.[42]

Chernyshevsky himself is confined within the circle of this biography, which is really a high-security prison describing several concentric circles, the first one being Chernyshevsky's own circular logic, the second one his son's biography of him, the third Fyodor's literary biography, and the fourth Nabokov's novel.

Escape proves impossible. Fyodor relies upon Strannolyubski to depict the scene of Chernyshevsky's arrest by secret police agent Rakeev in 1862:

> He sat down with the air of a guest; actually, he had come to arrest Chernyshevski. Again historical patterns come into that odd contact "which thrills the gamester in a historian" (Strannolyubski): this was the same Rakeev who as an embodiment of the government's contemptible scurry had whisked Pushkin's coffin out of the capital into posthumous exile.[43]

The "gamester in a historian" is first Nabokov, second Fyodor, and finally Chernyshevsky's son Alexander, the final form fate chooses for Chernyshevsky's nemesis. Alexander's pranks may be deciphered only through very attentive reading. A little example is the description of the writing equipment Chernyshevsky was provided with while a prisoner in the Peter and Paul Fortress in St. Petersburg, where he would later write *What Is to Be Done?*: "He was allowed a goose-quill pen, and one could write on a small green table with a sliding drawer, 'whose bottom, like Achilles' heel, had remained unpainted' (Strannolyubski)."[44] The knowledge Strannolyubski claims about the bottom of the desk would be impossible to anybody but, say, a small child who had actually visited Chernyshevsky in prison, observing the scene "with a child's care." Alexander Chernyshevsky would have been eight years old in 1862, so assuming family visits were permitted he could easily have ascertained this amusing information that he now transmits under the incognito of Strannolyubski.

Play in Nabokov's aesthetics is not mere mockery. True, Nabokov creates in *The Gift* a mock-biography of Chernyshevsky. True, too, he mocks Chernyshevsky's writing and role. The laughter is not without charity, however, and here Nabokov shows his final difference from Chernyshevsky.[45] Nabokov's art has everything to do with play. Life for Nabokov was a game of words and a game of worlds. One must play by the rules, however, and they necessitate a careful study of the world as it is: of nature, of people, of thought, of art. Careful study requires curiosity, which arouses an awareness of the sad beauty of things. From here spring playfulness and compassion.

> With great mastery and with utmost vividness of exposition (it might almost be taken for compassion) Strannolyubski describes his [Chernyshevsky's] installation in his Astrakhan

residence. No one met him with open arms, he was invited by no one, and very soon he understood that all the grandiose plans which had been his only support in exile must now melt away in an inanely lucid and quite imperturbable stillness.[46]

When Alexander, in verse, addresses his father's ghost, admonishing it not to "rail against life" but rather to "admit it's your fault you've been born with / An affectionate heart in your breast," we realize that Alexander himself is burdened with such a heart. And when Fyodor remarks that Alexander was one of the "unbalanced Russian poets of the woebegone sort" in whose poetry one detects "a flaw corresponding, it would seem, to something lacking in their lives, something that might have turned life into song," we recall that Alexander had flirted with insanity throughout his adult life, finally succumbing to it at the time of his miserable, lonely death in a foreign land.[47]

Returning to Alexander's terror of slipping into another dimension, I want to point out that the poor madman's fear has a second meaning. There is another Alexander Chernyshevsky in *The Gift*. Fyodor's friend Yasha Chernyshevsky has committed suicide, and Fyodor has befriended the grieving parents. The father's name is Alexander Chernyshevsky, making him the (apparently unrelated) namesake of Nikolai Chernyshevsky's son. It is in fact Alexander Chernyshevsky who indirectly inspires Fyodor with the idea of writing the biography of Chernyshevsky in the first place: Fyodor first conceives of his *Life of Chernyshevsky* when he sees in a Russian bookstore an issue of a Soviet chess magazine containing an article on "Chernyshevsky and Chess" and decides to buy it to amuse his friend Alexander Chernyshevsky. To sum up, there is an "outer" Alexander Chernyshevsky who exists in the same dimension as Fyodor, the author of the Chernyshevsky biography, and an "inner" Alexander Chernyshevsky who exists within the biography. If the inner Alexander slips into a different dimension, upon the event, say, of his miserable and lonely death, it must be into the outer dimension. And so the spirit of a son driven mad by the clash between his own dreamy transcendentalism and his father's militant materialism takes up residence in another world in the body of a father driven mad by grief for his son, who has committed suicide. The final irony is that, after passing through several phases of grief, the outer Alexander dies a misguided materialist. At first, in his desperate desire to regain contact with his dead son, Alexander has been seeing his ghost everywhere. Eventually he is interned in an asylum, where he begins to fight against the incursion of spirits into the world and dubs himself "Chairman of the Society for the Struggle with the Other World."[48] He eventually stops seeing his son's ghost and on his deathbed his last words are

> What nonsense. Of course there is nothing afterwards. . . . It is as clear as the fact that it is raining.
>
> And meanwhile outside the spring sun was playing on the roof tiles, the sky was dreamy and cloudless, the tenant upstairs was watering the flowers on the edge of her balcony, and the water trickled down with a drumming sound.

Alexander's mistake about the rain undercuts his newfound conviction that there is nothing after death and suggests that the question of his son Yasha's continued existence beyond death is still open. Meanwhile the inner Alexander disproves his father Nikolai Chernyshevsky's worldview by transcending to another dimension, where, in a sad irony, he is embodied in another grieving semi-lunatic.

The transcendental materialism of Nikolai Chernyshevsky's aluminum utopia is a cheap artistic effect, a "dishonest attempt to climb into the next dimension."[49] Nabokov shows what an honest attempt might look like: he has painstakingly constructed a novel whose protagonist Fyodor climbs (rather than slipping like poor Alexander) from the dimension of the protagonist to that of the author. He does it through the magic of a spiral structure, which is strictly speaking magical only from the vantage point of Fyodor's dimension. From our point of view this transition is a clever literary deception, achieved through a mind-boggling effort of artistry. So *The Gift* takes the form of a circle within spiral: Chernyshevsky's biography moves in a vicious circle, and he is trapped within. Fyodor's biography moves in a spiral, which Nabokov thought of as "spiritualized circle," eventually becoming his novel, and he achieves the sense of freedom that arises from artistic transcendence.[50]

Chernyshevsky was wrong: real roses are not better than painted ones; art is not inferior to life. The artless realization of literary ideals, though, particularly of bad ones, can destroy life. Unfortunately, Fyodor, too, was wrong:

We affirm that his book drew out and gathered within itself all the heat of his personality—a heat which is not to be found in its helplessly rational structures but which is concealed as it were between the words (as only bread is hot) and it was inevitably doomed to be dispersed with time (as only bread knows how to go stale and hard). Today, it seems, only Marxists are still capable of being interested by the ghostly ethics contained in this dead little book.[51]

When Nabokov wrote these words in the late 1930s, it was not only Marxists who were interested in rational egoism: Ayn Rand had revived it and adapted it for capitalism. Chernyshevsky's "ghostly ethics" had escaped the "dead little book" and taken possession of Ayn Rand's soul.

8

In the graveyard of bad ideas

Ayn Rand lived through a series of terrifying changes in her youth. She looked on helplessly as the Bolsheviks dispossessed her family, confiscating their business and real estate in Petrograd (now Saint St. Petersburg). She saw Lenin's Red Terror unfold, fled to the South during the civil war, returned to a hungry, cold Petrograd, and experienced political and social indoctrination at the University of Petrograd in the early 1920s. She had seen dystopia firsthand, and her literary beginnings root her firmly in the dystopic tradition: her novel *Anthem* (1938), which is extremely reminiscent of Evgeny Zamyatin's dystopian classic *We* (1921), describes a man's escape from a collectivist dictatorship. By the time she was writing *Atlas Shrugged* fifteen years later she had also evidently picked up the basics of doublespeak and doublethink from George Orwell.

This is not to say that Rand added nothing to the genre. The dystopian passages in *Atlas Shrugged* strike a tone of cynical invective that is not without originality. Some examples: a literary mediocrity, the darling of his age, is writing a novel called *The Heart is a Milkman*; when asked what it is about, he replies, "Frustration."[1] One of the chief collectivist "moochers," Lillian Rearden, comes to her husband Hank, wearing "an Empire garment of pale chartreuse, its pleated skirt streaming gracefully from its high waistline"; Hank "could not tell at first glance," remarks the narrator, "whether it was an evening gown or a negligee" and then, as if unable to resist bursting this petty enigma, immediately adds, "it was a negligee."[2] Another "vicious moocher" is Philip Rearden, whose eyes at the moment when Hank threatens to turn him out of his house are described as "filmy ovals that held no response to reality."[3] James Taggart's conversation with his wife just before she commits suicide is a mini-masterpiece of collectivist satire: "You loved me . . . because I was worthless?" she asks. "Well, what did you think you were?" "You loved me for being rotten?" "What else did you have to offer?"[4] Rand is entertaining when she mocks the collectivists. When she moves from the collectivist hangers-on to their totalitarian masters she is almost an interesting writer: Dr. Stadler, once John Galt's beloved physics professor, compromises himself more and more, until the chilling scene where America's new dictators pressure him to endorse "Project X." Project X, for those who could not make it past page 800, is a box that sends out sound waves powerful enough to obliterate any target. Impersonating scientific truth, Stadler goes on the radio and praises the horrific weapon as a guarantor of "permanent peace," a "harmonizer," which will eliminate war forever, dealing decisively with external as well as internal enemies.[5] The scene is an effective conclusion to the process of gradual corruption Rand had been evolving over many hundreds of pages.

Rand is persuasive in her case that the destruction of reason and logic must precede the destruction of freedom in a totalitarian regime. But having deconstructed the dystopia of collectivist dictatorship, she goes on to construct her own utopia, an Atlantis of Logic that places the entirety of human experience in reason's thrall. We find in the novel two applications of science, both originating with the theoretical physics of Dr. Stadler: one is meant to deliver mankind from toil, the other to deliver mankind into eternal slavery. The problem is that Galt's Gulch, the utopia built upon his perpetual motion machine, is not really free; its denizens are chained to logic as to a cliff in all they say or do. This is a cult of reason that subverts Rand's would-be Aristotelian framework, deceptively downgrading it into Plato's Republic. When the dust settles at the end of the novel and the utopians at Galt's Gulch are divvying up the world, Rand's victorious heroes read Aristotle, rejoicing in the fact that A=A. Rand seems not to comprehend that the very idea of utopia is Platonic, not Aristotelian. When you attempt to apply reason to spheres of experience that are inherently irrational, you create constraints and contradictions, and these are the crannies where a new tyranny puts down roots. Out of these contradictions arises the weirdest excess of Ayn Rand's style: robotic titans struggling to master their emotions, to force these emotions to proceed from logical thought.

A telling example of Rand's tone deafness that predates the writing of *Atlas Shrugged* is her infatuation with the American serial killer William Edward Hickman, who was to her an American "superman." In 1928, soon after Rand's arrival in the United States, Hickman was tried for the kidnapping and savage murder of Marion Parker, a twelve-year-old girl he had abducted from her school in Los Angeles. Hickman strangled her, slit her throat, dismembered, and finally disemboweled her. He said during his interrogation that he thought she had still been alive when he began to cut off her arms and legs. To collect ransom money from Marion's father, Hickman wrapped her corpse in blankets, wired her eyes open, stuffed a towel into her abdominal cavity to absorb blood, and propped her up in the passenger seat of his car. When Hickman drove up to collect the ransom, Mr. Parker could see his daughter sitting in the car with open eyes and fell for the ruse. Getting back into the car with the money, Hickman opened the door and pushed Marion's body out onto the street. The murderer was arrogant and defiant during his trial and cheerfully faced his sentence: execution by hanging.

Rand was so taken by Hickman's story that she used him as the prototype for the hero of a novel she never wrote that she wanted to call *The Little Street*. In her notebooks, Rand wrote with loathing about the "mob" that had formed around Hickman and reasoned that the public outcry was a reaction to his "daring challenge to society."[6] Hickman was "one of these rare, free, clear spirits" whom the mob cannot control. She valued his "remorselessness," "strength," "his calm, superior, indifferent, disdainful countenance," and "his immense, explicit egoism."[7] "A strong man," she reflected, "can eventually trample society under his feet. That boy was not strong enough. But is that his crime?" Clearly Rand valued strength, independence, pride, and egoism rising to the level of despotism, or, as she puts it, "extremism." Her use of the word "extremist" in describing Hickman is characteristic of the tradition of "Rakhmetovism" that Rand inherited from Russian culture: "If men were extremists," she writes, "they would follow each idea and feeling to its end, they would be faithful to their purposes and to themselves, they would be clear, straight, and absolute in everything. . . . This is what my book is going to say."[8] When she pivots from her observations on Hickman to her narrative plans in *The Little Street*, Rand seems not to notice that she is depicting the murderer as victim: "This case showed me how society can wreck an exceptional being, and then murder him for being the wreck that it itself has created. This will be the story of the boy in my book."[9] Not one word did Rand write about the actual victim of Hickman's crime, Marion Parker.

The serial killer Hickman entered into Rand's literary consciousness and became an essential component of the superhuman heroes of her future novels. Danny Renahan, the hero of *The Little Street*, was to have the "outside of Hickman," but not the inside. "A Hickman with a purpose. And without the degeneracy."[10] In her notes Rand emphasizes that Danny "does not understand, *because he has no organ for understanding*, the necessity, meaning or importance of other people." Symptomatically, he "has the true, innate psychology of a Superman. He can never realize and *feel* 'other people.'"[11] The quality Rand is adoring in her hero is psychopathy, the inability to feel empathy. At the end of *The Little Street*, Danny was to be tried for murdering his childhood pastor, convicted and sentenced to death. In court he would make a "scalding," "wild" speech of "condemnation."[12] Rand's idea that Danny's courtroom speech be "the very heart of the book" anticipates Howard Roark's courtroom speech in *The Fountainhead* and Hank Rearden's in *Atlas Shrugged*. On the first day of his trial, Rearden echoes the words of the extremist Sergei Nechaev at his own famous trial: "I do not recognize this court's right to try me."[13] Rand's prototypical hero is "superior to the mob," "stone-hard," "monstrously cruel," an "extreme 'extremist.'"[14] After sketching out her plans for *The Little Street*, Rand writes a brief motivational message to herself in her journal: "You must know how to control your moods and your mind. Be absolute master of yourself and your mind. How can you rule anybody or anything, if you can't rule your own mind? Be a tyrant—no compromises with yourself."[15] Rand is famous for her hatred of tyranny and for her love of freedom, but if the pursuit of personal freedom requires you to become a tyrant, then freedom is easily revalued into tyranny. Logic is a versatile instrument.

Rand's use of the word "Superman" to describe Danny recalls the superman Nietzsche had called for in *Thus Spake Zarathustra* (1891) who would recreate all values. Since her superhero is based upon an unrepentant murderer, he also recalls Dostoevsky's

Raskolnikov, who wanted to prove himself an "extraordinary man" by killing in cold blood without remorse. But Russian culture offers a more germane superhuman prototype: Rakhmetov, along with the line of terrorists he engendered. The hero of *The Fountainhead*, Howard Roark, is an extremist who blows up a building with a bomb, and the business Titans of *Atlas Shrugged* are no different. Ellis Wyatt sets fire to his oil wells. Francisco d'Anconia blows up his copper operations. On the eve of his corporate sabotage, he deliberately causes a selling panic in his company's stock and watches the panic spread through a wedding party, admiring the effects of "the impersonal breath of terror."[16] This last example, of financial terror, anticipates the activities of Rand's final hero, Alan Greenspan.

Since Rand's heroic personae were stitched together from the parts of living and fictional extremists, one wonders what effect her books might have on impressionable readers. In an essay entitled "The Psycho-Epistemology of Art" Rand boasts that many fans of *The Fountainhead* had reported to her that they had resolved dilemmas in their own lives by asking, "What would Roark do in this situation?"—whereupon "faster than their mind could identify the proper application of all the complex principles involved, the image of Roark gave them the answer."[17] This is the precise method of brainwashing through idolatry that I have been describing in this book: it works by switching off critical thinking in order to facilitate emotional identification with an idol. In another essay on the nature of fiction Rand argues that a rational person reads a novel in order to find there "an image in whose likeness he will re-shape the world and himself. Art gives him that image; it gives him the experience of seeing the full, immediate, concrete reality of his distant goals."[18] This is precisely how a human being yields up his volition, hollows out his personality, and allows himself to become a "Manchurian Candidate," triggered to perform whatever action is required. Roark is a terrorist who blows up a huge building in New York City, so a reader who asks, "What would Roark do?" and then allows Roark's image to guide his actions might do just about anything. In this sense "Roarkism" and "Galtism" are but a further evolution of "Rakhmetovism."

It would be good to do as Rand (and Galt) always urged and "check your premises." At a sales conference, shortly before the publication of *Atlas Shrugged*, a salesman asked Rand to summarize her philosophy while standing on one leg. The game Rand accepted the challenge. Balancing on one foot she uttered, "Metaphysics—objective reality; Epistemology—reason; Ethics—self-interest; Politics—capitalism."[19] With the exception of Rand's substitution of capitalism for socialism, her objectivism is precisely the same as Chernyshevsky's rational egoism, a phrase she very nearly uses in *The Virtue of Selfishness*: "The Objectivist ethics proudly advocates and upholds *rational selfishness*."[20] Having embraced such a thing, Rand immediately feels bound to try to defend it, assuring the reader that "there is no conflict of interests among men who do not desire the unearned, who do not make sacrifices nor accept them, who deal with one another as *traders*, giving value for value."[21] The problem here is that it may be perfectly rational for a selfish operator to try and cheat another selfish operator out of some "value." Machiavelli was the very soul of rationality, as was Sade, and it is easy to imagine what they might say about this. If the first operator rationally understands that he can claim (steal) the second's "unearned" valuables and get away with it, what will stop him? Reason will not. Selfishness will not. Suspecting the weakness of this position, Rand tries to shore it up with the notion of "justice," but this is an irrational appeal to an outside arbiter, whether God or state or some abstraction, and as such has nothing to do with our two traders. In her essay "The Objectivist Ethics," Rand asserts that "happiness is that state of consciousness which proceeds from the achievement of one's values."[22] As proof of her claim she quotes from Galt's intolerable seventy-page speech in *Atlas Shrugged*:

> Happiness is a state of non-contradictory joy—a joy without penalty or guilt, a joy that does not clash with any of your values and does not work for your own destruction. . . . Happiness is possible only to a rational man, the man who desires nothing but rational goals, seeks nothing but rational values and finds his joy in nothing but rational actions.[23]

Chasing after her own literary creations in an unvirtuous circle, Rand often appealed to her fictions for support. But quoting Galt flies in the face of the very logic that the two of them purport to champion. By the rules of her own objectivism, logic was to link concepts to percepts, but percepts must be based on empirical reality, not on literary conceits.

For Rand, the basis of humanity must be reason: from reason flowed egoism and from egoism capitalism.[24] Art, too, was supposed to spring from reason:

> The art of any given period or culture is a faithful mirror of that culture's philosophy. If you see obscene, dismembered monstrosities leering at you from today's esthetic mirrors—the aborted creations of mediocrity, irrationality and panic—you are seeing the embodied, *concretized* reality of the philosophical premises that dominate today's culture. . . . It is a frightening sight, but it has a certain didactic value: those who do not wish to surrender their future to the mercy and power of unfocused gargoyles can learn from them what swamp is their breeding ground and what disinfectant is needed to fight them. The swamp is modern philosophy; the disinfectant is reason.[25]

This passage, as Nabokov might say, substitutes its own victim for the one the author has intended. It also seems to be lifted from Chernyshevsky's *What Is to Be Done?* where Kirsanov and Lopukhov discuss the drainage of swamps in Vera's second dream.[26]

And since we are speaking of Vera's dreams, her fourth one furnished Rand with the blueprints for her own utopia. Chernyshevsky's utopia of aluminum, labor, and copulation prepares the way for Galt's Gulch, a utopia of Rearden's Metal, the Galt engine and, well, copulation. In *Atlas Shrugged* as in *What Is to Be Done?* rational egoists perpetually assure one another that any generous things they happen to do are not to be construed as acts of "charity" or "favors" but merely side effects of their pursuit of selfish ends. A nice example of this is the scene where Francisco d'Anconia asks John Galt whether Galt's guest, Dagny, may spend her last night with him. When Galt answers no, all three are pleasantly relieved that Galt has refused to "fall to the lowest possible stage of altruism," sacrificing his own desires (Dagny's sexual favors) to those of his friend. Dagny reflects that if Galt had handed her over to Francisco, "faking his greatest feeling out of existence," then she, too, would have ended up lying to (sleeping with) Francisco, whom she no longer loves, and then Francisco would have stumbled into a permanent "fog of a counterfeit reality," a "fraud staged by the two who were dearest to him and most trusted."[27] As in *What Is to Be Done?* altruism is strictly forbidden here, or, in the dictatorial phrase of Galt's, "Nobody stays here by faking reality *in any manner whatever.*"[28]

Rand's biography offers an interesting comment on the sin of faking reality: her affair with her disgraced high priest, Nathaniel Branden. At the start of their extramarital relationship, she and Branden had convened a meeting with Rand's husband Frank O'Connor and Branden's wife Barbara, and had demanded an afternoon each week for sex. The spurned spouses took it as well as any traumatized cult members might, but it was injurious and humiliating to them. Writing *Atlas Shrugged*, Rand would read passages aloud to her little following, who playfully (too playfully) called themselves the "Collective." Among them were Branden, O'Connor, Barbara Branden, Leonard Peikoff, and Alan Greenspan. One can only imagine the effect that the love scene in the Gulch must have had upon its first audience. Ayn had at first dedicated the book to Branden. (She would later rededicate it to her husband O'Connor.) Clearly, all that praise of "self-esteem" on the pages of *Atlas Shrugged* was a tribute to Branden, an early popularizer of the importance of self-esteem, which he taught as one of the subfields of objectivism at the Nathaniel Branden Institute. Rand fancied Branden and herself to be superheroes, Titans, real-life versions of Dagny and Galt. It may have been heroic, at least by objectivist rules, to save Barbara Branden and O'Connor from a "counterfeit" reality by revealing the affair to them; but when it came time several years later for Branden to choose between an aging Rand and Patrecia, the younger woman he had fallen in love with (and would soon marry), Rand was completely unwilling to allow him to choose his happiness, insisting that he stay with her, that is, that he "fake reality." When he refused, she became hysterical, insulted him, slapped him in the face, and excommunicated him. Jeff Walker begins *The Ayn Rand Cult* with a dramatization of the scene: "In a furious rage, the 63-year-old woman glared at the handsome young man seated in front of her, and in a choked voice, with a heavy Russian accent, placed a curse on his penis."[29] Rand wrote a thunderous article about Branden's "betrayal" of objectivism in her *Objectivist Newsletter*, and also published a letter of denunciation, signed by Greenspan, Peikoff, and the other "collectivists." This denunciation is a rather striking example of people faking reality and thereby becoming the thing they most hate.

Rand faked reality. The Collective faked reality. What about her favorite heroes? Hank Rearden and Dagny Taggart present an interesting case. Though Hank is married, he detests his wife Lillian and eventually falls in love with Dagny. While he would like to be free to live with Dagny, he feels a little guilty toward Lillian, and this guilt makes him vulnerable to his collectivist enemies, who blackmail him and force him to gift Rearden Metal to the state. In this way he betrays everything he has ever done or dreamed of doing. Rearden is a giant among men but not quite as Titanic as John Galt, who would never dream of feeling guilt or shame. When Dagny falls in love with Galt, Rearden immediately gives her up, declaring that "if love means one's final, irreplaceable choice, then he [Galt] is the only man you've ever loved." This revision of history defies logic. Dagny's dramatic reply, a "half-gasp, half-scream," consists of one word: "Yes!"[30] With that word the deal is sealed. Even though Galt's commandment is "Nobody stays here by faking reality *in any manner whatever*," Dagny and Hank do in fact stay in Galt's Gulch precisely by "faking reality." They rewrite the past, just like any thorough-going collectivist rewrites history, and their romance goes right down the "memory hole."

Given his dictatorial tone, a gift from his author, it is natural that Galt should eventually hijack the airwaves of the People's Republic of the United States and announce to his countrymen that the supreme dictator, Mr. Thompson, would not be addressing them that night: "His time is up," says Galt, "I have taken over."[31] Galt and his fellow utopians are waiting for the total collapse of the infrastructure so that they can pick up the pieces and assume control. As the novel ends, "Midas" Mike Mulligan, vulture banker extraordinaire, is sitting in front of a map, drawing up plans to swoop down, and gobble up, almost at no cost, invaluable assets along the train routes: "New York—Cleveland—Chicago . . . New York—Philadelphia . . . New York . . . New York . . . New York . . ."[32] It was Galt and his industrialist cohorts who caused the collapse when they "stopped the motor" of the nation by blowing up their factories, oil fields, and mines and withdrawing. I do not claim that they were wrong to withdraw, but by doing so they brought about a situation that was extremely advantageous to them and in the process became vulture capitalists.

Since Chernyshevsky's novel *What Is to Be Done?* became an explicit and even state-mandated exemplar for the writers of socialist realism behind the Iron Curtain, it is more than just coincidental that Ayn Rand's capitalist realism, inspired by the same source, resembles Soviet "construction novels." Like socialist realism in the USSR, Rand's capitalist realism champions industrial action as a force that will humanize the universe. Work alone justifies mankind. Labor must turn nature into a scientific utopia for heroic, rational humanity. In their toil, Rand's heroes exhibit a gargantuism that recalls Chernyshevsky's barge-hauling Rakhmetov: Rearden, for instance, is "too tall for those around him."[33] Francisco d'Anconia explains the novel's title to Rearden, whom he is radicalizing in one of the book's key scenes: "If you saw Atlas, the giant who holds the world on his shoulders, if you saw that he stood, blood running down his chest, his knees buckling, his arms trembling . . . what would you tell him to do?" The correct answer to Francisco's question is "shrug"—in other words, drop the world of collectivist "moochers" and go join the other gods on Olympus, here called Galt's Gulch. John Galt himself becomes a Titan when he invents a perpetual motion machine that harnesses the unlimited static electricity from the earth's atmosphere. Chernyshevsky, please recall, was obsessed in his youth with inventing a perpetual motion machine, so Galt realizes Chernyshevsky's dream. In Francisco's allegory, the Promethean Galt climbed a mountain in order to discover "the fountain of youth," which he intended to bring down to men."[34] Instead, "after centuries of being torn by vultures in payment for having brought to men the fire of the gods, he broke his chains and he withdrew his fire—until the day when men withdraw their vultures."[35] Rand amusingly substitutes a collectivist vulture for the standard eagle in her version of the myth of Prometheus.

To Dagny the train terminal her ancestor Nathaniel Taggart built looks like a "temple" or "cathedral," and the deity of this cathedral, the giant statue of Nat Taggart, dominates the concourse.[36] Nat Taggart is an apology for John D. Rockefeller, who built first an oil empire and then a train empire to move his oil around. Like Rockefeller, Taggart pursued his ambitions relentlessly, and his contemporaries resented him for being a "successful bandit." Yet "no penny of his wealth had been obtained by force or fraud; he was guilty of nothing, except that he earned his own fortune and never forgot that it was his." True, he seems to have murdered a state legislator who tried to revoke a charter granted him, but nothing could be proven in court. After that, Rand's narrator chortles, he "had no trouble with legislators."[37] The notion suggested here, that murder is justifiable when its victims are "looters" who stand in the capitalist's way, is at the very heart of *Atlas Shrugged*. Key here is the name of Rand's actress, Kay (i.e., "the key") Ludlow. Ludlow joins the capital strike in Galt's Gulch, quitting the theater in the "outer world," where she was compelled to "play nothing but symbols of depravity."[38] The notion of Ludlow joining a strike in Colorado can only indicate the most infamous strike in the history of American capitalism, which occurred at a Rockefeller coal mine in Ludlow, Colorado, in 1913–14. When the miners went on strike for safer and more humane working conditions (an eight-hour work day, the right not to use the company store, fair compensation for labor, etc.), management kicked them and their families out of company housing and into the bitter cold of a Colorado winter. When the striking coal miners made a tent settlement there, hired thugs assaulted them with Gatling guns. That did not quell the strike, and the Governor of Colorado called in the National Guard, whose wages were paid by the Rockefellers. The result was more gunfire, and then the tent settlement went up in flames. Some twenty-four men, women, and children were killed, leading to the worst public relations disaster that even the Rockefellers had ever seen.

Rand turns these historical facts on their heads. Instead of oppressed workers striking against capitalist goons who have bought and bullied the government into criminal complicity, it is the capitalists who go on strike in *Atlas Shrugged*. It is they, not the laborers, who are oppressed, by unfair laws favoring the miserable, mediocre masses of "sloppy bums" (Rand's name for workers) rather than the job creators. In his long speech at the end of the novel, Galt attacks physical laborers as a nearly useless atavism of the middle ages:

How many tons of rail do you produce per day if you work for Hank Rearden? Would you dare to claim that the size of your paycheck was created solely by your physical labor and that those rails were the product of your muscles? The standard of living of [a] blacksmith is all that your muscles are worth; the rest is a gift from Hank Rearden.

Apparently unsure whether his insults have been sufficiently outrageous, Galt opines that laborers are practically useless: "Physical labor as such can extend no further than the range of the moment. The man who does no more than physical labor consumes the material value-equivalent of his own contribution to the process of production, and leaves no further value, neither for himself nor others." These are not nice words, but "such is the nature of the 'competition' between the strong and the weak of the intellect."[39] It is said that killers tend to dehumanize their victims in order to be psychologically capable of their crimes. Rand is about to murder some workers, and so we see her agent Galt stripping away their humanity. This is just the brand of "extremism" and psychopathy that we saw in Rand's response to the Marion Parker murder. The murderer is made out to be victim, the actual victim being callously ignored, and over it all hangs a dollar sign, three feet tall and made of solid gold, the celestial body and guiding light of our capitalist utopia. Rand's composer in utopia, Richard Halley, chooses to play for the tone-deaf industrialist Ken Danagger, not for the parasite laborers and their collectivist managers on the outside.[40] The phrase "tone-deaf" is generally applicable.

Early in the novel, walking through Manhattan, Dagny pauses before a bookstore window display of a new novel, *The Vulture is Molting*: "The novel of our century," "The penetrating study of a businessman's greed."[41] *Atlas Shrugged*, which reconstitutes businessmen into virtuous vultures, is the antidote to this imaginary novel. When Dagny and Hank are out in Colorado buying up idle machinery on the cheap from "doubtful owners," Dagny feels "like a scavenger."[42] And then there is the scene at the end of the novel where the utopianists of Galt's Gulch are preparing to snatch up the distressed assets of the crumbling People's Republic of the United States of America. The interplay of these "vulture" scenes is amusing, but not intentionally so. The impression one gets is that the words have rebelled against their careless author and are setting up meanings of their own behind her back, or, as it were, right under her beak. The reason for this mutiny of words is presumably Rand's unjustified hubris in attempting to refashion the world through the power of the word.

And it is not merely words but key concepts that rebel. Rand employs some choice mockery in depicting the State Science Institute that refuses to acknowledge the safety and indeed superiority of Rearden's Metal. This Institute, however, is a straw man she has rigged up, almost, it would seem, to divert the reader's attention from the fact that the heroes she worships—the inventors of the miracles that will save humanity from squalor and poverty—are technocrats. Rand's capitalists value industrial efficiency over all other things. There is a jarring Taylorism in

Atlas Shrugged that does not sit well with the ideal of freedom. Rand's attitude toward the methods and ideals of technocracy is naively uncritical. Upon discovering John Galt's miraculous motor, Dagny asks Hank, "Do you know what that motor would have meant, if built?" His Tayloristic reply is: "About ten years added to the life of every person in this country—if you consider how many things it would have made easier and cheaper to produce, how many hours of human labor it would have released for other work, and how much more anyone's work would have brought him." Then he adds a thought worthy of Lenin himself: "That motor could have set the whole country in motion and on fire. It would have brought an electric light bulb into every hole." The scene ends as the sun goes down over the impoverished environs of Galt's abandoned factory. Dagny peers melodramatically out a factory window, moaning, shuddering, and dropping her head as the wan lights begin to flicker in the impoverished houses of the former factory workers: it is the light not of electric light bulbs but of tallow candles.[43] Lenin's motto of "electrification of the entire country" comes to mind: the Soviet leaders, too, were enamored of Taylorism and attempted to implement it in their five-year plans and in efficiency-improving production methods.

Rand seems to be a technocrat and, by extension, a collectivist, without knowing it. Her own words reveal the contradictions in her thinking. The word "obscenity" is an interesting example. The "Equalization of Opportunity Bill" that forces Hank Rearden to sell his mining operations for pennies on the dollar is unequivocal proof that the United States of *Atlas Shrugged* have devolved into a collectivist tyranny. When the collectivists take his mines away, Rearden tells himself that this is an example of "an obscenity of evil which contaminates the observer," for there is "a limit to what it is proper for a man to see."[44] In this scene Rand is probably depicting her own revulsion and fear as a witness to her father's disenfranchisement at the hands of the Bolshevists. But in another scene Rand uses this selfsame word, "obscenity," precisely in order to contaminate the observer, her reader. She describes Rearden's lust for Dagny Taggart, whom he plans to "reduce . . . to a body" and teach "an animal's pleasure" as he yearns "to see [her] wonderful spirit dependent upon the obscenity of [her] need." "What would you be like," he thinks, looking at the object of his obscene lust, "if I knocked your head back, if I threw you down in that formal suit of yours, if I raised your skirt"—Dagny looks up, and Rearden looks away and must wait a couple dozen pages before answering these indelicate questions for himself in one of Rand's famous love-as-rape scenes.[45] When the slapping and clawing is over and the moon rises over the scene, Rearden tells Dagny that he does not love her but has merely wanted her "as one wants a whore," "as the bitch you are." While he has nothing but admiration for her business talents, it is "the obscenity of your talent at an animal's sensation of pleasure" that he prefers.[46] Why, one wonders, are Rearden's rape fantasies and violent copulation with Dagny not beyond the "limit to what it is proper" to see? Is the compulsion of rape not, like the compulsion of capital looted by the state, "an obscenity of evil which contaminates the observer"? Not, Rand might reply, when Dagny desires precisely to be "raped" in this manner, when she is exchanging value for value with Rearden in the marketplace of violent sexual fantasies. Rand and her heroes apparently compensate for the state's "obscene" violence against them by inflicting a stylistic violence upon the reader, who may not desire an initiation into the secrets of Ayn Rand love. Rearden later apologizes for his abuse of Dagny and accepts his loss of her to Galt as just punishment, but I cannot help believing him when he exults in calling her a whore and disbelieving his auto-flagellation of repentance.

When Rearden's wife Lillian demands that he cut off his affair with Dagny, he refuses, seeing "the obscenity of letting impotence hold itself as virtue and damn the power of living as a sin."[47] Hank admits to his wife that his lover is Dagny and refuses to give her up, and suddenly feels a new freedom, as if "some weight . . . had been torn off his shoulders,"[48] the freedom of an Atlas "shrugging" off the burden of conscience. In the absence of conscience, though, there can be no empathy. Dagny, even more so than Rearden, is "completely incapable of experiencing a feeling of fundamental guilt."[49] Rand herself gleefully kills off an entire train full of passengers—men, women, and small children—because they (the grown-ups at any rate) uphold "cowardly little obscenities to the effect that all businessmen were scoundrels."[50] The gloating enumeration of these doomed persons in their various sleeper cars along with their sins against objectivism is every bit as chilling as the scene demonstrating the genocidal potential of "Project X." What obscenity really signifies in a Rand novel is the reduction of people to robots through a hollowing out of their moral core.

Through this technocratic wonderland the robotic heroes move with electric grace until the circuit is tripped, and they lurch to a stop. It is then that we discern most clearly that they are indeed machines. Dagny Taggart presents a striking example: "It seemed to her for a moment as if she, too were a precision instrument of high technology, left without electric current."[51] And again: "Dagny let the paper slip to the floor. She sat, bent over, her head on her arms. She did not move, but the strands of hair, hanging down to her knees, trembled in sudden jolts once in a while."[52] Some of the jerkiness was intended, but that will hardly be of comfort to a reader trying to process phrases like "indifferent astonishment," for this time Rand herself is the robot.[53] John Galt looks "as if he were poured [a calque from the Russian; Rand means 'cast'] out of metal." What kind of metal? Most likely "an aluminum-copper alloy."[54] The aluminum takes us right back to *What Is to Be Done?* We have seen that Francisco and Rearden prove able to turn their love for Dagny off the instant they understand that she has fallen for Galt. This is because Rand's robots apply logic to emotions: if Dagny and Galt find their "ultimate values" in each other then there is logically no room for anyone else in the equation. Jealousy is irrational, and surrendering your mind to the irrational is choosing death over life, and so on. "Did it ever occur to you, Miss Taggart," Galt asks Dagny, "that there is no conflict of interests among men, neither in business nor in trade nor in their most personal desires—if they omit the irrational from their view of the possible and destruction from their view of the practical? There is no conflict, and no call for sacrifice, and no man is a threat to the aims of another—if men understand that reality is an absolute not to be faked."[55]

Jeff Walker shows in *The Ayn Rand Cult* that "Rand bullied her inner circle, the Collective, who in turn bullied the students of Objectivism, who in turn bullied possible converts."[56] The literary fruit of such a cult of personality is the deadly dictatorial tone in the novel. Her "collectivists," to whom she read *Atlas Shrugged* aloud, were too cowed to point out the mistakes that persisted in her English, to say nothing of her crimes of tone. And so the calques, contretemps, and solecisms accumulated. Francisco's last Spanish ancestor threw a glass of wine in the face of "the lord of the Inquisition" and then escaped to South America before he could be seized.[57] The "Collectivists" did not tell Rand that the job title is "Grand Inquisitor." Nor did they mention to her that English speakers do not "wash" their teeth. And if they were afraid to tell her that the idiom is to "brush" one's teeth, they were certainly in no state to object to the tyrannical excesses of *Atlas Shrugged*, as when Galt loses his philosophical cool and begins to insult humanity in jarring, juvenile words: "Take a look around you, you savages . . . you grotesque little atavists."[58] Nor, we can be sure, did anybody in her circle object when she read to them the following outrage against freedom: "I have foreshortened the usual course of history and have let you discover the nature of the payment you had hoped to switch to the shoulders of others."[59] The payment, by the way, is death: death to the looters, death to the irrational. Galt spends a long time reviling those "mystics" who value the irrational. He says that their secret desire is destruction and death and describes them as "a conspiracy against the mind, which means: against life and man."[60] "Every dictator is a mystic," says Galt, "and every mystic is a potential dictator. . . . What he seeks is power over reality and over men's means of perceiving it."[61] But Rand herself sought just that power.

Rand was a mystic, though she did not suspect it. In her mystery cult she made sacrifices at the Altar of Reason. The "vicious looters" and "grotesque little atavists" who would not bow down to reason, who would not put the irrational in themselves to death—these Rand herself ritualistically murdered in her fiction. Rand was the Oracle of Reason, and her acolytes from the Collective took her prophesies to the people. After *Atlas Shrugged* the deluded Rand expected a total transformation of the world. She waited in vain. For her efforts all she got was the devastating Whittaker Chambers review I mention in the Introduction. She began quoting John Galt. She wrote an essay titled "Is Atlas Shrugging?" She became more reclusive and abused drugs. Finally she released her last literary hero and final weapon, Alan Greenspan, into reality to implement objectivism as economic policy. Now there is mysticism for you.

In 1929 The American Tobacco Company hired one of the inventors of public relations, Edward Bernays, to con women into smoking cigarettes. This was at a time when smoking was considered scandalously unfeminine; but Bernays, a nephew of Sigmund Freud's, consulted with psychologists, who informed him that women are natural smokers thanks to the laws of oral fixation and penis envy. Bernays created a media frenzy by populating the Easter Parade in New York City with attractive young women smoking cigarettes, which they called "torches of freedom." Bernays spread photographs of these women and their freedom torches around the world, and the tobacco industry's profits soared. For much of *Atlas Shrugged* Dagny searches longingly for the manufacturer of a delicious brand of cigarettes she has stumbled upon. She asks her favorite cigarette vendor, who has a stand in Taggart Terminal, if he has ever come across the brand. Though he is an expert on cigarettes, he has never seen this particular brand. As a consolation prize, though, the vendor produces a little rhapsody on cigarette smoking: "I like cigarettes, Miss Taggart. I like to think of fire held in man's hand. Fire, a dangerous force, tamed at his fingertips."[62] In short, torches of freedom. Fire donated to mere mortals by the Prometheans among us. She finally discovers that the desired cigarettes are manufactured by the Mulligan Tobacco Company in Galt's Gulch. In the Gulch, when Dagny sees Galt's perpetual motion machine, she falls into a technocratic reverie, thinking of all of the future Atlases, from whose shoulders Galt's motor would lift the burden of inefficient labor, "adding hours, days and years of liberated time to their lives, be it an extra moment to lift one's head from one's task and glance at the sunlight, or an extra pack of cigarettes bought with the money saved from one's electric bill."[63] By the time Rand contracted lung cancer, the tobacco industry had known about the perils of cigarette smoking for decades, but they covered up the evidence, and their customers died unnecessary, agonizing deaths by the millions. In the scene where Galt, Hugh Akston, and the other conspirators attempt to enlist Dagny in their secret society, they are all smoking Mulligan cigarettes emblazoned with the gold dollar sign. One supposes that, like their creator, they all eventually succumbed to lung cancer. Unfettered capitalism is no more a utopia than the chained collective. The vulture will always come home to roost.

Acknowledgments

I would like to express my gratitude to my friends Alan Lorefice, Alexander Demyanov, and Joel Gardner for their interest and good humor during our many conversations about this book. Wellesley College supported my research with two grants. I also want to thank Ieva Galinyte, my excellent research assistant. I am deeply indebted to Katia Kapovich and Philip Nikolayev for invaluable editing help. My parents Andrew D. Weiner and Sonja Hansard-Weiner read my manuscript and made very useful suggestions. Most of all I thank my wife, Jenette Restivo. This book is dedicated to her.

Notes

Introduction

1 Vladimir Nabokov, "On Learning Russian," *Wellesley Magazine* 29, no. 4 (April 1945): 191–92.

2 John Maynard Keynes, *Essays in Persuasion* (London: MacMillan, 1931), 383.

3 Irina Paperno, *Chernyshevsky and the Age of Realism: A Study in the Semiotics of Behavior* (Stanford: Stanford University Press, 1988), 197. See also in Paperno, *Chernyshevsky*, 29–37.

4 Paperno, *Chernyshevsky*, 195.

5 In Andrew M. Drozd, *Chernyshevskii's What Is to Be Done? A Reevaluation* (Evanston, IL: Northwestern University Press, 2001), 9.

6 In Drozd, *A Reevaluation*, 10.

7 Paperno, *Chernyshevsky*, 218.

8 Drozd, *A Reevaluation*, 10.

9 Ayn Rand, "Basic Principles of Literature," in *The Romantic Manifesto: A Philosophy of Literature*, Second Revised Edition (New York: Signet, 1975), 72.

10 "William Buckley on Ayn Rand," Charlie Rose, PBS, WNET, New York City, Jun 16, 2003, television.

11 Anne C. Heller, *Ayn Rand and the World She Made* (New York: Nan A Talese, 2009), 286.

12 Whittaker Chambers, "Big Sister Is Watching You," *National Review* 4, no. 25 (1957): 597.

13 "William Buckley on Ayn Rand," Charlie Rose, PBS, WNET, New York City, Jun 16, 2003, television.

14 Ibid.

15 Heller, *Ayn Rand and the World She Made*, 286.

16 In Jennifer Burns, *Goddess of the Market: Ayn Rand and the American Right* (New York: Oxford University Press, 2009), 279.

17 Alan Greenspan, *Age of Turbulence: Adventures in a New World* (New York: Penguin, 2008), 52–53.

18 In John B. Judis, *William F. Buckley Jr., Patron Saint of the Conservatives* (New York: Simon and Schuster, 2001), 163.

19 Jon Ward, "He Found the Flaw?" *The Washington Times*, October 24, 2008.

20 Ibid.

21 David Corn, "Alan Shrugged," *Mother Jones*, October 24, 2008.

22 Yves Smith, *Econned* (New York: Palgrave Macmillan, 2010), 135.

23 Smith, *Econned*, 135.

24 Ibid., 5.

25 Ibid., 20.

26 See Daniel Altman, "Managing Globalization," in *Q & A* with Joseph E. Stiglitz, Columbia University and *The International Herald Tribune*, October 11, 2006 05:03 a.m., available online at http://economistsview.typepad.com/economistsview/2006/10/joseph_stiglitz.html.

27   Nouriel Roubini, "Who Is to Blame for the Mortgage Carnage and Coming Financial Disaster? Unregulated Free Market Fundamentalism Zealotry," *EconoMonitor*, March 19, 2007.

28   Greenspan, *Age of Turbulence*, 52.

29   Thomas Frank, "The Job Creators Strike Out," *Harpers Magazine*, November 23, 2011.

30   See Thomas Frank, "The Job Creators Strike Out," *Harpers Magazine*, November 23, 2011.

31   http://ari.aynrand.org/media-center/press-releases/2010/01/21/atlas-shrugged-sets-a-new-record.

32   Harriet Rubin, "Ayn Rand's Literature of Capitalism," *The New York Times*, September 15, 2007.

33   Burns, *Goddess of the Market*, 279.

34   Rand Paul, "Rand Paul on Ayn Rand and His Name," online video clip, YouTube, October 5, 2009.

35   Mackenzie Weinger, "7 Pols Who Praised Ayn Rand," *Politico*, April 26, 2012.

36   Mark Sanford, "Mark Sanford on Ayn Rand," *Newsweek*, October 21, 2009.

Chapter 1

1   See Joseph Frank, *Dostoevsky. The Stir of Liberation. 1860-1865* (Princeton: Princeton University Press, 1986), 44–45.

2   Nikolai Karamzin, "Bednaia Liza," in *Izbrannye proizvedeniia*, vol. 2 (Moscow: Khodozhestvennaia Literatura, 1964).

3   See Joseph Frank, *The Seeds of Revolt* (Princeton: Princeton University Price, 1979), 81–91.

4   Nikolai V. Gogol, *Sobranie sochinenii v semi tomakh*, vol. 6 (Moscow: Khudozhestvennaia literatura, 1966), 427.

5   Gogol, *Sobranie sochinenii v semi tomakh*, vol. 6, 259–60.

6   V. G. Belinsky, "Letter to Nikolai Gogol," in *Documents in Russian Literature*, trans. Daniel Field, http://academic.shu.edu/ russianhistory/index.php/Vissarion_Belinsky%2C_Letter_to_Gogol.

7   Ibid.

8   Dostoevsky, Fyodor M. *Polnoe sobranie sochinenii v tridtsati tomakh*, vol. 18, ed. G. M. Fridlender (Leningrad-St. Petersburg: Nauka, 1972), 128–29. In Frank, *The Stir of Liberation*, 77.

9   Frank, *The Seeds of Revolt*, 187.

10   In Andrzej Walicki, *History of Russian Thought* (Stanford: Stanford University Press, 1979), 159.

11   In Walicki, *History of Russian Thought*, 160.

12   Frank, *The Seeds of Revolt*, 246.

13   Ibid., 254.

14   Ibid.

15   V. I. Lenin, *Polnoe sobranie sochinenii v 55 tomakh*, 5th ed. (Moscow: Izdatel'stvo politicheskoi literatury, 1958–65), vol. 7, 438, footnote.

16   In J. H. Seddon, *The Petrashevtsy: A Study of the Russian Revolutionaries of 1848* (Manchester: Manchester University Press, 1985), 79.

17   In Seddon, *The Petrashevtsy*, 132.

18   See, Seddon, *The Petrashevtsy*, 209.

19   Ibid.

20   See his letter to a Polish friend in V. Evgrafova, ed., *Filosofskie i obshchestvenno-politicheskie proizvedeniia petrashevtsev* (Moscow: Gosudarstvennoe izdatel'stvo politcheskoi literatury, 1953), 488–502.

21   See James H. Billington, *Fire in the Minds of Men: Origins of the Revolutionary Faith* (New York: Basic Books, 1980), 586, note 75; *Literaturnoe nasledstvo*, LXIII, 1956, 1 71–2; and Seddon, *The Petrashevtsy*, 43.

22   See Seddon, *The Petrashevtsy*, 212.

23 See Billington, *Fire in the Minds of Men*, 586, n. 75: "Speshnev advocated that the central committee have three coequal subordinate bodies: Jesuitical, propagandistic, and revolutionary."

24 Feliks Moiseevich Lur'e, *Nechaev: Sozidatel' razrusheniia*, in *Zhizn' zamechatel'nykh liudei* series (Moscow: Molodaia gvardiia, 2001), 84.

25 Seddon, *The Petrashevtsy*, 208–09.

26 Aleksei Dolinin, *Dostoevskii v vospominaniiakh sovremennikov*, 2 vols (Moscow, Khudozhestvennaia literature, 1964), I: 172, cited in Frank, *The Seeds of Revolt*, 269–70.

27 Lur'e, *Nechaev*, 85.

28 Joseph Frank, *A Writer in His Time* (Princeton: Princeton University Press, 2009), 179. "We will be with Christ"; "A bit of dust."

Chapter 2

1 Nikolai Chernyshevsky, *Chto delat' (What Is to be Done?),* vol. 1 of *Sobranie sochinenii v piati tomakh* (Moscow: Pravda, 1974), 13. I will from now on refer to this edition as *SSVPT.*

2 In Paperno, *Chernyshevsky*, 26.

3 In Drozd, *A Reevaluation*, 13.

4 In Drozd, *A Reevaluation*, 11.

5 Ibid., 11–12. I have slightly modified Drozd's translation.

6 In Paperno, *Chernyshevsky*, 27.

7 N. V. Volsky, *Encounters with Lenin*, trans. Paul Rosta and Brian Pearce (London and New York: Oxford University Press, 1968), 63.

8 See Drozd, *A Reevaluation*, 6–9.

9 Vladimir Nabokov, *The Gift: A Novel* (New York: Vintage Books, 1991), 276–77.

10 Adam Ulam, *Prophets and Conspirators in Prerevolutionary Russia* (New Brunswick and London: Transaction Publishers, second edition, 1998), 99.

11 Ibid., *Prophets and Conspirators*, 109.

12 Ibid., 105.

13 Chernyshevsky, *SSVPT*, vol. 4, 7.

14 Ibid., 7, 9.

15 In Drozd, *A Reevaluation*, 21.

16 Ralph Matlaw, introduction to *Belinsky, Cheryshevsky, and Dobrolyubov: Selected Criticism* (New York: Dutton, 1962), xv, cited in Drozd, *A Reevaluation*, 21.

17 In Drozd, *A Reevaluation*, 44.

18 Chernyshevsky, *SSVPT*, vol. 1, 103–04.

19 Ibid., 125.

20 Ibid., 159.

21 Ibid., 161.

22 Ibid., 187.

23 Ibid., 192.

24 Ibid., 194.

25 Ibid., 195.

26 Ibid., 220.

27 Ibid., 221.

28 Ibid., 222.

29 Ibid.

30 Ibid., 230–31.

31 Ibid., 247.

32 Ibid., 248.

33 Ibid., 248–49.

34 For Chernyshevsky's use of hagiography, see Drozd, *A Reevaluation*, 41–42.

35 Chernyshevsky, *SSVPT*, vol. 1, 270.

36 Ibid., 273.

37 Ibid., 270.

38 Ibid., 274.

39 Ibid., 279.

40 Ibid., 274.

41 Adam Smith, *An Inquiry into the Nature and Causes of the Wealth of Nations* (New York: The Modern Library, 1937), 423.

42 Chernyshevsky, *SSVPT*, vol. 1, 284.

43 Ibid., 9.

44 Ibid., 308.

45 Ibid., 323.

46 Ibid., 365–66.

47 Ibid., 375.

48 Ibid.

49 Ibid., 376.

50 Ibid., 383.

51 Ibid., 384.

Chapter 3

1 Dostoevsky, *PSS*, vol. 18, 35.

2 Ibid., 36.

3   Ibid.

4   Ibid., 37.

5   Ibid.

6   Ibid., 79. In Frank, *The Stir of Liberation*, 77.

7   Ibid., 94. In Frank, *The Stir of Liberation*, 77. I have modified Frank's translation.

8   Ulam, *Prophets and Conspirators*, 110.

9   Dostoevsky, *PSS*, vol. 21, 25–26.

10   Dolinin, *Dostoevskii v vospominaniiakh sovremennikov*, vol. 1, 319–21.

11   Nabokov, *The Gift*, 267–68.

12   Dostoevsky, *PSS*, vol. 5, 387.

13   Ibid., 185.

14   Ibid.

15   Ibid., 194.

16   Ibid., 195.

17   Dostoevsky, *PSS*, vol. 21, 24.

18   See Frank, *The Stir of Liberation*, 128.

19   Dostoevsky, *PSS*, vol. 5, 124.

20   Ibid., 111.

21   Ibid., 110.

22   Ibid.

23   Ibid., 105.

24   Chernyshevsky, *SSVPT*, vol. 1, 192.

25   Dostoevsky, *PSS*, vol. 5, 102.

26   Ibid., 120.

Chapter 4

1 Drozd, *A Reevaluation*, 114.

2 Ibid., 10.

3 Claudia Verhoeven, *The Odd Man Karakozov: Imperial Russia, Modernity, and the Birth of Terrorism* (Ithaca and London: Cornell University Press, 2009), 20.

4 Verhoeven, *Karakozov*, 21.

5 Paul Avrich, *Bakunin and Nechaev* (London: Freedom Press, 1987), 7–8.

6 Verhoeven, *Karakozov*, 20.

7 Ibid., 58.

8 In Verhoeven, *Karakozov*, 58.

9 See Verhoeven, *Karakozov*, 60.

10 Verhoeven, *Karakozov*, 60.

11 Avrich, *Bakunin and Nechaev*, 7.

12 Verhoeven, *Karakozov*, 60.

13 Drozd, *A Reevaluation*, 10. See also Drozd's endnote:

Several officials, among them Count Murav'ev, wanted to bring Chernyshevskii back to Saint St. Petersburg to stand trial for plotting the tsar's assassination. However, Chernyshevskii was already safely isolated and cooler heads prevailed. The government contented itself merely by blaming Chernyshevskii and his novel for having a destructive influence. This claim was a part of the official sentence pronounced upon the Karakozovites. (note 85, 194)

14 Chernyshevsky, *SSVPT*, vol. 1, 278, 282.

15 Verhoeven, *Karakozov*, 41.

16 Ibid., 147.

17 Sergei Nechaev, "Catechism of a Revolutionary", http://www.hist.msu. ru/ER/Etext/nechaev.htm.

18 Chernyshevsky, *SSVPT*, vol. 1, 280.

19 Drozd, *A Reevaluation*, 115.

20 Avrich, *Bakunin and Nechaev*, 5.

21 Ibid., 6.

22 See Philip Pomper, *Sergei Nechaev* (New Brunswick, NJ: Rutgers University Press, 1979), 55–56.

23 See Pomper, *Sergei Nechaev*, 57–58.

24 Ibid., 63.

25 In Pomper, *Sergei Nechaev*, 65.

26 See Pomper, *Sergei Nechaev*, 66.

27 Ibid., 72.

28 Ibid., 77.

29 In Pomper, *Sergei Nechaev*, 96.

30 See Lur'e, *Nechaev*, 85.

31 Pomper, *Sergei Nechaev*, 79.

32 In Pomper, *Sergei Nechaev*, 82.

33 Pomper, *Sergei Nechaev*, 81.

34 See Pomper, *Sergei Nechaev*, 86–87.

35 Ibid., 73–74.

36 Pomper, *Sergei Nechaev*, 94.

37 See Pomper, *Sergei Nechaev*, 108–10.

38 Pomper, *Sergei Nechaev*, 109.

39   See Pomper, *Sergei Nechaev.*, 94–95.

40   Pomper, *Sergei Nechaev*, 112.

41   See Pomper, *Sergei Nechaev*, 104.

42   See Pomper's wonderful recreation of the murder in Pomper, *Sergei Nechaev*, 112–15.

43   Pomper, *Sergei Nechaev*, 115.

Chapter 5

1   V. V. Vinogradov, "Primechaniia," Dostoevsky, *PSS*, vol. 7, 323.

2   See *Karakozov*, 99–103. According to Verhoeven, the fact that Raskolnikov's friend Razumikhin (incorrectly) suspects Raskolnikov of being a political conspirator is directly attributable to the Karakozov case (102).

3   Dostoevsky, *PSS*, vol. 29, part I, 260.

4   Joseph Frank, *The Miraculous Years* (Princeton: Princeton University Press, 1996), 403.

5   Dostoevsky, *PSS*, vol. 29, bk. 1, 260 (February 10, 1873).

6   Ibid., 215 (May 30, 1871).

7   Dostoevsky, *PSS*, vol. 12, 129.

8   Dostoevsky, *PSS*, vol. 10, 238.

9   Ibid.

10   Ibid., 239–40.

11   Ibid., 239.

12   In Joseph Frank, *The Miraculous Years* (Princeton: Princeton University Press, 1996), 402.

13   In Frank, *The Miraculous Years*, 402.

14 Fyodor Dostoevsky, *Demons*, trans. Robert A. Maguire (London and New York: Penguin, 2008), 484.

15 Nikolai Chernyshevsky, *Art's Aesthetic Relationship to Reality*, *Sobranie sochinenii v piati tomakh*, vol. 4, ed. IU. S. Melenent'iev (Moscow: Pravda, 1974), 74, 117.

16 See Pisarev's article of 1865, "Pushkin i Belinskii."

17 Dostoevsky, *PSS*, vol. 10, 395.

18 Ibid., 373.

19 Our holy Russia.

20 Dostoevsky, *PSS*, vol. 10, 373, 499.

21 See Sergei Bulgakov, who remarked that Stavrogin is actually but "an empty space" where the ideological devils find the "inspiration of evil." Sergii Bulgakov, "Russkaia tragediia," in vol. 2 of *Sochineniia v dvukh tomakh*, ed. I. B. Rodnianskaia (Moscow: Nauka, 1993), 522.

22 Dostoevsky, *PSS*, vol. 10, 203.

23 Ibid., 27.

24 See, for example, Dostoevsky, *PSS*, vol. 11, 279. See also Verhoeven, *Karakozov*, 100.

25 Dostoevsky, *PSS*, vol. 10, 198.

26 Ibid.

27 Ibid., 199.

28 Ibid., 200–01.

29 Frank, *The Miraculous Years*, 404.

30 Dostoevsky, *PSS*, vol. 10, 236.

31 Ibid., 272.

32 Ibid., 311.

33 Ibid., 322.

34 Pomper, *Sergei Nechaev*, 202.

35   Dostoevsky, *PSS*, vol. 10, 452.

36   Dostoevsky, *PSS*, vol. 29, bk. 1, 214.

Chapter 6

1   See Pomper, *Sergei Nechaev*, 137–39.

2   Ibid., 140–41.

3   Pomper, *Sergei Nechaev*, 143.

4   Ibid., 145–46.

5   Ibid., 146–47.

6   Ibid., 147–52.

7   Ibid., 155.

8   In Frank, *The Miraculous Years*, 440–41.

9   Pomper, *Sergei Nechaev*, 154–61.

10 Ibid., 178–82.

11 Ibid., 204.

12 Ibid., 206.

13 Ibid., 214–15.

14 See Lur'e, *Nechaev*, 296.

15 Pomper, *Sergei Nechaev*, 121.

16 Valentinov (Volsky), *Encounters with Lenin*, 64. Note: I have altered
    the translation here, making it more literal.

17 Valentinov (Volsky), *Encounters with Lenin*, 67.

18 Mariia Moiseevna Essen, "Vstrechi s Leninym nakanune i v dni
    pervoi russkoi revoliutsii," in *Voprosy istorii*, 1955, no. 1, 26–32,
    http://leninism.su/memory/1735-vstrechi-s-leninym-nakanune-i-v-
    dni-pervoj-russkoj-revolyuczii.html.

19 Joseph Frank, *Through the Russian Prism: Essays on Literature and Culture* (Princeton: University of Princeton Press, 1990), 187.

20 Valentinov (Volsky), *Encounters with Lenin*, 67–68.

21 See Richard Pipes, "The Origins of Bolshevism," *Revolutionary Russia*, ed. Richard Pipes (Cambridge, MA: Harvard University Press), 1968, 35.

22 Orlando Figes, *A People's Tragedy: A History of the Russian Revolution* (London: Viking, 1996), 389–90. See also Robert Payne who writes that "as Lenin had ... modeled himself on Chernyshevsky's Rakhmetov so [Lenin's lover] Inessa [Armand] had modeled herself on the novel's heroine Vera." Robert Payne, *The Life and Death of Lenin* (New York: Simon and Schuster, 1964), 235.

23 Pipes, "The Origins of Bolshevism," 33–34.

24 Ibid., 36–37.

25 Valentinov (N. V. Volsky), *Encounters with Lenin,* 63–64. Note: I have slightly altered the translation here, making it more literal.

26 G. V. Plekhanov, *N.G. Chernyshevskii* (St. Petersburg: Shipovnik, 1910), 16–17.

27 Lars T. Lih, *Lenin Rediscovered: "What Is to Be Done?" in Context* (Leiden, The Netherlands: Koninklijke Brill NV, 2006), 14.

28 See Jerrold Siegel, *Marx's Fate: The Shape of a Life* (University Park, Pennsylvania: The Pennsylvania State University Press, 1993), 248.

29 V. I. Lenin, *What Is to Be Done?*, trans. Joe Fineberg and Gerorge Hanna (London: Penguin Books, 1988), 119.

30 Lenin, *What Is to Be Done?*, 107.

31 Ibid., 137.

32 Ibid., 143–44.

33 Ibid., 145.

34 Ibid., 147.

35 G. V. Plekhanov, "Zametki publitsista. Novye pis'ma o taktike i bestaktnosti," in *Sochineniia*, vol. 15 (Moscow and Leningrad:

Gosudarstvennoe izdatel'stvo, 1926), http://az.lib.ru/p/ plehanow_g_w/text_1907_novye_pisma.shtml

36 G. V. Plekhanov, "God na rodine," in *Polnoe sobranie statei i rechei v dvukh tomakh*, volume 2 (Paris: J. Povolozky, 1921), 267.

37 V. I. Lenin, "Dve taktiki sotsial-demokratii v demokraticheskoi revoliutsii," in *Polnoe sobranie sochinenii v 55 tomakh* (Moscow: Izdatel'stvo politicheskoi literatury, 1958), 5th edition, vol. 11, 47.

38 Lih, *Lenin Rediscovered*, 17–18.

39 Emphasis as in the original. Leon Trotsky, *Our Political Tasks* (London: Publications, 1980).

40 https://www.marxists.org/archive/trotsky/1904/tasks/ch05.htm.

41 Ibid.

42 Ibid.

43 Richard Stites, *Revolutionary Dreams: Utopian Vision and Experimental Life in the Russian Revolution* (New York and Oxford: Oxford University Press, 1989), 27.

44 Stites, *Revolutionary Dreams*, 27.

Chapter 7

1 Alexander Dolinin, *Istinnaia zhizn' pisatelia Sirina: raboty o Nabokove* (St. Petersburg: Akademicheskii proekt, 2004), 106.

2 Nabokov, *The Gift*, 207.

3 Nabokov, *The Gift*, from the "Foreword."

4 Nabokov, *The Gift*, 168.

5 See Alexander Dolinin, "Nabokov's Time Doubling: from *The Gift* to *Lolita*," *Nabokov Studies* 2 (1995), 14, footnote 34. Dolinin mentions John Malmstead's idea that the name Mortus in *The Gift* indicates Georgy Adamovich through its reference to the Death's-head hawkmoth (genus *Acherontia*), which in Russian is known both as "mertvaia golova" ("Dead Head") and as "adamova golova" ("Adam's Head").

6 Nabokov, *The Gift*, 169.

7 Letter quoted in Dolinin, *Istinnaia zhizn' pisatelia Sirina*, 107. See also Dolinin's remarks on Nabokov's careful use of documented facts in his characterization of Chernyshevsky, 131–32.

8 See Dolinin, *Istinnaia zhizn' pisatelia Sirina*, 107.

9 Nabokov, *The Gift*, 265.

10 Ibid., 276–77.

11 Ibid., 249.

12 Ibid., 289.

13 Ibid., 299.

14 Ibid., 217.

15 Ibid., 222.

16 Ibid., 225.

17 Ibid., 244.

18 Ibid., 216.

19 Ibid., 237.

20 Ibid., 246.

21 Ibid., 247.

22 Ibid., 282.

23 G. V. Plekhanov, *N. G. Chernyshevskii* (St. Petersburg: Shipovnik, 1910), 16–17.

24 Paperno, *Chernyshevsky*, 220.

25 Nabokov, *The Gift*, 257.

26 Ibid., 259.

27 Ibid., 260.

28 Ibid.

29 Ibid., 296.

30 Ibid.

31 Ibid., 297.

32 Ibid., 297–98.

33 Ibid., 298.

34 Ibid.

35 Ibid., 217.

36 Ibid., 220.

37 Ibid., 300.

38 Ibid., 212.

39 Ibid.

40 Ibid., 202–03.

41 Ibid., 245.

42 Ibid., 244.

43 Ibid., 269.

44 Ibid., 272.

45 For more on Fyodor's concealed compassion in his treatment of Chernyshevsky, see Brian Boyd, *Vladimir Nabokov, The Russian Years* (Princeton: Princeton University Press, 1990), 458.

46 Nabokov, *The Gift*, 293.

47 Ibid., 298, 296.

48 Ibid., 91.

49 Ibid., 3.

50 See Vladimir Nabokov, *Speak, Memory* (New York: Vintage International, 1989), 275: "The spiral is a spiritualized circle. In the spiral form, the circle, uncoiled, has ceased to be vicious; it has been set free."

51 Nabokov, *The Gift*, 281–82.

Chapter 8

1 Ayn Rand, *Atlas Shrugged* (New York: Dutton, 1992), 134.

2 Rand, *Atlas Shrugged*, 304.

3 Ibid., 470.

4 Ibid., 902–03.

5 Ibid., 825.

6 Ayn Rand, *The Journals of Ayn Rand*, ed. David Harriman (New York: Penguin, 1997), 36.

7 Rand, *The Journals of Ayn Rand*, 37.

8 Ibid., 41–42.

9 Ibid., 38.

10 Ibid., 27.

11 Ibid.

12 Ibid., 28.

13 Rand, *Atlas Shrugged*, 477.

14 Rand, *The Journals of Ayn Rand*, 26.

15 Ibid., 48.

16 Rand, *Atlas Shrugged*, 422.

17 Ayn Rand, "The Psycho-Epistemology of Art," in *The Romantic Manifesto: A Philosophy of Literature* (New York: Signet, 1975), 10.

18 Ayn Rand, "Art and Sense of Life," in *The Romantic Manifesto: A Philosophy of Literature* (New York: Signet, 1975), 28.

19 Nathaniel Branden, *Judgment Day: My Years with Ayn Rand* (Boston: Houghton Mifflin, 1989), 229.

20 Ayn Rand, "The Objectivist Ethics," in *The Virtue of Selfishness*, ed. Ayn Rand and Nathaniel Branden (New York: The New American Library, 1964), 34.

21 Rand, "The Objectivist Ethics," 34.

22 Ibid., 31.

23 Ibid., 32.

24 "Brief Summary," *The Objectivist*, September 1971, 1089.

25 "Basic Principles of Literature," *The Objectivist*, August 1968, 503–04.

26 For Rand's debt to Chernyshevsky, see D. Barton Johnson, "Strange Bedfellows: Ayn Rand and Vladimir Nabokov," *The Journal of Ayn Rand Studies* 2, no. 1 (2000): 47–67.

27 Rand, *Atlas Shrugged*, 795.

28 Ibid., 797. The italics are Rand's.

29 Jeff Walker, *The Ayn Rand Cult* (Chicago and La Salle, IL: Open Court, 1999), 1.

30 Rand, *Atlas Shrugged*, 860.

31 Ibid., 1009.

32 Ibid., 1167.

33 Ibid., 28.

34 Ibid., 178.

35 Ibid., 517.

36 Ibid., 59.

37 Ibid., 60.

38 Ibid., 784.

39 Ibid., 1064–65.

40 Ibid., 782.

41   Ibid., 66.

42   Ibid., 518.

43   Ibid., 290–91.

44   Ibid., 215.

45   Ibid., 204–05.

46   Ibid., 254.

47   Ibid., 530.

48   Ibid., 531.

49   Ibid., 87.

50   Ibid., 606.

51   Ibid., 953.

52   Ibid., 69.

53   Ibid., 79.

54   Ibid., 701.

55   Ibid., 798.

56   Walker, *The Ayn Rand Cult*, 16.

57   Rand, *Atlas Shrugged*, 91.

58   Ibid., 1049.

59   Ibid., 1052.

60   Ibid., 1047.

61   Ibid., 1045.

62   Ibid., 61.

63   Ibid., 730.

Works cited

Altman, Daniel. "Managing Globalization: Q & A with Joseph Stiglitz." October 11, 2006. *The International Herald Tribune.* LexisNexis Academic. Web. http://www8.gsb.columbia.edu/faculty/jstiglitz/sites/jstiglitz/files/Economist's%20View_%20Joseph%20Stiglitz%20Q%20%26%20A.pdf.

"*Atlas Shrugged* Sets a New Record!" Ayn Rand Institute. N.p., January 21, 2010. Web. https://ari.aynrand.org/media-center/press-releases/2010/01/21/atlas-shrugged-sets-a-new-record.

Avrich, Paul. *Bakunin and Nechaev.* London: Freedom Press, 1987. Print.

Belinsky, V. G. "Letter to Nikolai Gogol." Translated by Daniel Field. *Documents in Russian History.* Web. http://academic.shu.edu/russianhistory/index.php/Vissarion_Belinsky,_Letter_to_Gogol.

Billington, James H. *Fire in the Minds of Men: Origins of the Revolutionary Faith.* New York: Basic Books, 1980. Print.

Boyd, Brian. *Vladimir Nabokov, The Russian Years.* Princeton: Princeton University Press, 1990. Print.

Branden, Nathaniel. *Judgment Day: My Years with Ayn Rand.* Boston: Houghton Mifflin, 1989.

Bulgakov, Sergei. "Russkaia tragediia." Vol. 2 of Sochineniia v dvukh tomakh. Edited by I. B. Rodnianskaia. Moscow: Nauka, 1993. Print.

Burns, Jennifer. *Goddess of the Market: Ayn Rand and the American Right.* New York: Oxford University Press, 2009. Print.

Chambers, Whittaker. "Big Sister Is Watching You." *National Review* 4, no. 25 (1957). Web. http://www.nationalreview.com/article/213298/big-sister-watching-you-whittaker-chambers.

Chernyshevsky, Nikolai. *Sobranie sochinenii v piati tomakh.* Edited by IU. S. Melenent'iev. Moscow: Pravda, 1974. Print.

Corn, David. "Alan Shrugged." *Mother Jones.* October 24, 2008. Web. http://www.motherjones.com/politics/2008/10/alan-shrugged.

Dolinin, Aleksei. *Dostoevskii v vospominaniiakh sovremennikov.* 2 Vols. Moscow: Khudozhestvennaia literatura, 1964. Print.

Dolinin, Alexander. *Istinnaia zhizn' pisatelia Sirina: raboty o Nabokove.* Petersburg: Akademicheskii proekt, 2004. Print.

Dolinin, Alexander. "Nabokov's Time Doubling: From *The Gift* to *Lolita.*" *Nabokov Studies* 2 (1995): 3–40. Print.

Dostoevsky, Fyodor M. *Demons.* Translated by Robert A. Maguire. London and New York: Penguin, 2008. Print.

Dostoevsky, Fyodor M. *Polnoe sobranie sochinenii v tridtsati tomakh.* Edited by G. M. Fridlender. Leningrad-St. Petersburg: Nauka, 1972. Print.

Drozd, Andrew M. *Chernyshevskii's "What Is to Be Done?" A Reevaluation.* Evanston: Northwestern University Press, 2001. Print.

Evgrafova, V., ed. *Filosofskie i obshchestvenno-politicheskie proizvedeniia petrashevtsev.* Moscow: Gosudarstvennoe izdatel'stvo politcheskoi literatury, 1953. Print.

Figes, Orlando. *A People's Tragedy: A History of the Russian Revolution.* London: Viking, 1996. Print.

Frank, Joseph. *Dostoevsky. The Stir of Liberation. 1860-1865.* Princeton: Princeton University Press, 1986. Print.

Frank, Joseph. *The Miraculous Years.* Princeton: Princeton University Press, 1996. Print.

Frank, Joseph. *The Seeds of Revolt.* Princeton: Princeton University Press, 1979. Print.

Frank, Joseph. *Through the Russian Prism: Essays on Literature and Culture.* Princeton: University of Princeton Press, 1990. Print.

Frank, Joseph. *A Writer in His Time.* Princeton: Princeton University Press, 2009. Print.

Frank, Thomas. "The Job Creators Strike Out." *Harpers Magazine.* November 23, 2011. Web. http://harpers.org/blog/2011/11/the-job-creators-strike-out/.

Gogol, Nikolai V. *Sobranie sochinenii v semi tomakh.* Moscow: Khudozhestvennaia literatura, 1966. Print.

Greenspan, Alan. *Age of Turbulence: Adventures in a New World.* New York: Penguin, 2008. Print.

Heller, Anne C. *Ayn Rand and the World She Made*. New York: Nan A. Talese, 2009. Print.

Johnson, D. Barton. "Strange Bedfellows: Ayn Rand and Vladimir Nabokov." *The Journal of Ayn Rand Studies* 2, no. 1 (2000): 47–67. Print.

Judis, John B. *William F. Buckley, Jr.: Patron Saint of the Conservatives*. New York: Simon & Schuster, 1998. Print.

Karamzin, Nikolai. "Bednaia Liza." In *Izbrannye proizvedeniia*. Vol. 2. Moscow: Khodozhestvennaia literatura, 1964. Print.

Keynes, John Maynard. *Essays in Persuasion*. London: MacMillan, 1931. Print.

Lenin, V. I. *Polnoe sobranie sochinenii v 55 tomakh*. 5th ed. Moscow: Izdatel'stvo politicheskoi literatury, 1958. Print.

Lenin, V. I. *What Is to Be Done?* Translated by Joe Fineberg and Gerorge Hanna. London: Penguin Books, 1988. Print.

Lih, Lars T. *Lenin Rediscovered: "What Is to Be Done?" in Context*. Leiden, the Netherlands: Koninklijke Brill NV, 2006. Print.

Lur'e, Feliks Moiseevich. *Nechaev: Sozidatel' razrusheniia*. In *Zhizn' zamechatel'nykh liudei* series. Moscow: Molodaia gvardiia, 2001. Print.

Matlaw, Ralph. Introduction to *Belinsky, Chernyshevsky, and Dobrolyubov: Selected Criticism*. New York: Dutton, 1962. Print.

Nabokov, Vladimir. *Speak, Memory*. New York: Vintage International, 1989. Print.

Nabokov, Vladimir. *The Gift: A Novel*. New York: Vintage Books, 1991. Print.

Nechaev, Sergeï G. "Catechism of a Revolutionary". Web. http://www.hist.msu.ru/ER/Etext/nechaev.htm

Paperno, Irina. *Chernyshevsky and the Age of Realism: A Study in the Semiotics of Behavior*. Stanford: Stanford University Press, 1988. Print.

Pipes, Richard. "The Origins of Bolshevism." In Richard Pipes (ed.), *Revolutionary Russia*, 26–52. Cambridge, MA: Harvard University Press, 1968. Print.

Pisarev, D. I. "Pushkin i Belinskii." In IU. S. Sorokin (ed.), *Sochineniia v chetyrekh tomakh*, Vol. 3, 306–417. Moscow: Khudozhestvennaia literatura, 1956. Print.

Plekhanov, G. V. "God na rodine." In *Polnoe sobranie statei i rechei 1917–1918 v dvukh tomakh*. Paris: J. Povolozky, 1921. Print.

Plekhanov, G. V. *N.G. Chernyshevskii*. St. Petersburg: Shipovnik, 1910. Print.

Plekhanov, G. V. "Zametki publitsista. Novye pis'ma o taktike i bestaktnost." In *Sochineniia*. Vol. 15. Moscow and Leningrad: Gosudarstvennoe izdatel'stvo, 1926. Web. http://az.lib.ru/p/plehanow_g_w/text_1907_novye_pisma.shtml.

Pomper, Philip. *Sergei Nechaev*. New Brunswick, NJ: Rutgers University Press, 1979. Print.

Rand, Ayn. *Atlas Shrugged*. New York: Dutton, 1992. Print.

Rand, Ayn. *The Journals of Ayn Rand*. Edited by David Harriman. New York: Penguin, 1997. Print.

Rand, Ayn. "Art and Sense of Life." In *The Romantic Manifesto: A Philosophy of Literature*, 24–34. New York: Signet, 1975. Print.

Rand, Ayn. "Basic Principles of Literature." In *The Romantic Manifesto: A Philosophy of Literature*, 71–90. Second Revised Edition. New York: Signet, 1975. Print.

Rand, Ayn. "The Psycho-Epistemology of Art." In *The Romantic Manifesto: A Philosophy of Literature*, 3–13. New York: Signet, 1975. Print.

Rand, Ayn. "The Objectivist Ethics." In Ayn Rand and Nathaniel Branden (eds), *The Virtue of Selfishness*, 13–39. New York: The New American Library, 1964. Print.

Rand, Paul. "Rand Paul on Ayn Rand and His Name." Online video clip. *YouTube*. October 5, 2009. Web. https://www.youtube.com/watch?v=oD-R_OeP6tU.

Riurikova, B. "Lenin o Chernyshevskom i ego romane 'Chto delat'?" *Voprosy literatury*, 8 (1957): 126–34. (1957). Print.

Robert, Payne. *The Life and Death of Lenin*. New York: Simon and Schuster, 1964, 235. Print.

Roubini, Nouriel. "Who Is to Blame for the Mortgage Carnage and Coming Financial Disaster? Unregulated Free Market Fundamentalism Zealotry." *EconoMonitor*. March 19, 2007. Web. http://www.economonitor.com/nouriel/2007/03/19/who-is-to-blame-for-the-mortgage-carnage-and-coming-financial-disaster-unregulated-free-market-fundamentalism-zealotry/.

Rubin, Harriet. "Ayn Rand's Literature of Capitalism." *The New York Times*. September 15, 2007. Web. http://www.nytimes.com/2007/09/15/business/15atlas.html?_r=0

Sanford, Mark. "Mark Sanford on Ayn Rand." *Newsweek*. October 21, 2009. Web. http://www.newsweek.com/mark-sanford-ayn-rand-81147

Seddon, J. H. *The Petrashevtsy: A Study of the Russian Revolutionaries of 1848*. Manchester: Manchester University Press, 1985. Print.

Smith, Adam. *An Inquiry into the Nature and Causes of the Wealth of Nations*. New York: The Modern Library, 1937. Print.

Smith, Yves. *ECONned: How Unenlightened Self Interest Undermined Democracy and Corrupted Capitalism*. Basingstoke: Palgrave Macmillan, 2011. Print.

Stites, Richard. *Revolutionary Dreams: Utopian Vision and Experimental Life in the Russian Revolution*. New York and Oxford: Oxford University Press, 1989. Print.

Trotsky, Leon. *Our Political Tasks*. London: New Park Publications, 1980. Print.

Ulam, Adam. *Prophets and Conspirators in Prerevolutionary Russia*. New Brunswick and London: Transaction Publishers. Second edition. 1998. Print.

Valentinov (Volsky), Nikolai. *Encounters with Lenin*. Translated by Paul Rosta and Brian Pearce. Foreword by Leonard Schapiro. London and New York: Oxford University Press, 1968. Print.

Verhoeven, Claudia. *The Odd Man Karakozov: Imperial Russia, Modernity, and the Birth of Terrorism*. Ithaca and London: Cornell University Press, 2009. Print.

Walicki, Andrzej. *History of Russian Thought*. Stanford: Stanford University Press, 1979. Print.

Walker, Jeff. *The Ayn Rand Cult*. Chicago and La Salle, IL: Open Court, 1999. Print.

Ward, Jon. "He found the flaw?" *The Washington Times*. October 24, 2008. Web. http://www.washingtontimes.com/blog/potus-notes/2008/oct/24/he-found-flaw/.

Weinger, Mackenzie. "7 Pols Who Praised Ayn Rand." *Politico*. April 26, 2012. Web. http://www.politico.com/story/2012/04/7-pols-who-praised-ayn-rand-075667.

"William Buckley on Ayn Rand." Charlie Rose. PBS. WNET, New York City. Jun 16, 2003. Television.

Index